New Political Eco
Exchange Rate Pc
and the Enlargem

Contributions to Economics

www.springer.com/series/1262

Christian H. Fahrholz

New Political Economy
of Exchange Rate Policies
and the Enlargement
of the Eurozone

With 12 Figures and 9 Tables

Physica-Verlag

A Springer Company

Series Editors
Werner A. Müller
Martina Bihn

Author
Dr. Christian H. Fahrholz
Department of Politics and Management
University of Konstanz
Universitätsstraße 10
78464 Konstanz
Germany
E-mail: christian.fahrholz@uni-konstanz.de

ISSN 1431-1933
ISBN 10 3-7908-1761-9 Physica-Verlag Heidelberg New York
ISBN 13 978-3-7908-1761-4 Physica-Verlag Heidelberg New York

Physica-Verlag is a part of Springer Science+Business Media GmbH

springer.com

© Physica-Verlag Heidelberg 2007

Typesetting: Camera ready by the author
Cover: Erich Kirchner, Heidelberg
Production: LE-TEX, Jelonek, Schmidt & Vöckler GbR, Leipzig

SPIN 11820482   Printed on acid-free paper – 134/3100 – 5 4 3 2 1 0

To my family

Preface

The work with this study has been extensive as well as exciting. Help, support and encouragement from several persons have promoted the completion of this work.

First of all, I would like to thank my supervisor Prof. Dr. Michael Bolle for his inimitable way of teaching and guiding me in my quest to reach a thorough understanding of knowledge and science, and for his valuable comments during the creation of this thesis. Likewise, I thank my secondary supervisor Prof. Dr. Gerald Schneider for his thoughtful insights, Prof. Dr. Carsten Helm for his willingness to discuss the initial ideas of my game-theoretic models and Jan Rübel and Vera Tröger for discussing further mathematical issues with me.

I am very grateful to my colleagues (and former fellow-travellers) at the Jean Monnet Centre of Excellence. Special thanks go to Achim Kemmerling with whom I have shared an office during the last few years. This time has proven to be an estimable symbiotic relationship. Thanks also to Shana Moffett-Heyder for helping me with my English.

This work has benefited greatly from my collaboration within the research project *"The Eastward Enlargement of the Eurozone"* (*Ezoneplus*). Many ideas in this thesis have been developed as a result of that collaboration. Financial and further support have been provided by the DFG-Graduate College *"The New Europe"* and the *Berlin Graduate School of Social Sciences*.

At last, I thank Dörte Nedderhut for her love, understanding, and patience—patience is a virtue.

Konstanz, *Christian H. Fahrholz*
June 2006

Contents

X   Contents

1

Introduction

"Erstens kommt es immer anders, zweitens als man denkt." – This German proverb means that things never turn out the way you think they will, and it has a rather fatalistic connotation to it. To many observers there is a good deal of risk attached to the European enlargement process, specifically with regard to the Central Eastern Europe (CEE). However, the admittance of eight of these Central Eastern European Countries (CEECs) to the European Union (EU)just seemingly puts an end to risks involved in this enlargement process. The next issue to be dealt with is the CEECs' run up to the European Economic and Monetary Union (EMU). Those who deem the eastward enlargement of the eurozone as an incidental process of European integration rejoice too soon. The CEECs' path towards adopting the euro as legal tender might prove to be a bumpy ride for the European enlargement process.

This work analyses exchange-rate policy in the course of the eurozone's eastward enlargement. The formation of exchange-rate policies in the CEECs during their Exchange-Rate Mechanism II (ERM II) pass through is of particular research interest. New EU-member countries[1] joined the EU in May 2004. The CEECs are committed to entering ERM II – an integral part of the Maastricht criteria – soon afterwards. As there is no opt-out clause for the new EU-members, they are expected to join the EMU around the beginning of 2007.

Exchange-rate policies, particularly with respect to the prescribed fixed exchange-rate regimes (so-called soft pegs), in ERM II are generally crisis-prone. During its predecessor in the European Monetary

---

[1] Cyprus, the Czech Republic, Estonia, Hungary, Latvia, Lithuania, Malta, Poland, Slovakia and Slovenia. When analysing hereafter, prospective or new member countries, then CEECs are meant. Cyprus and Malta are not considered, because these countries do not fit into the subsequently developed argument.

System (EMS), the according soft pegs of its members proved prone to
speculative attacks, which plunged European exchange-rate affairs into
considerable turmoil. The consequences of malfunctioning policy formation with regard to exchange-rate arrangements became especially
evident in the EMS-crisis of 1992–93. Erroneous policies as well as economic shocks also put transitory exchange-rate regimes of individual
CEECs in ERM II at risk. However, such risks and their repercussions
on the economic and the political formation cannot be exclusively assigned to a particular CEEC. The reason is that contagion generates
external effects in terms of spreading defaults, thus, putting the entire
European enlargement process at risk.

Research is conducted along the lines of political economy because it
makes allowance for interdependent decision-making in economic and
political systems. Additionally, political economy strives for establishing a coherent and consistent actor-centric approach. Exchange-rate
policy, as a research topic, lies at the crossroads of economics and politics. Hence, this issue is just right for a political-economic analysis.

Generally, the performance of one country's exchange-rate policy engenders external effects on the policy formation of other countries. Correspondingly, such external effects can deteriorate the overall functioning of the European exchange-rate relations, thereby endangering the
stability of the EMU-enlargement process. At the same time, there is
no easy way of internalizing such impending risks in European matters.
At first glance, exchange-rate questions are economic issues. Nevertheless, there are governments which make decisions on policies affecting
the durability of fixed exchange-rate regimes. These actors' decisions
are not only guided by economic reasoning, but most notably, by political concerns. Aggregating voter preferences and thus facing a specific
voter demand for a specific economic policy performance curtails politicians' capacities for preserving the long-run stability of soft pegs. With
regard to external effects, the well-known two-level metaphor suggests
that any negotiated intergovernmental solution to the internalization
problem has to recognize that national executives adhere to their constituencies' preferences.

One of the challenges involved in the EMU-enlargement process is
that ERM II fosters disturbing incentives, which were not initially envisaged by its founders. ERM II and other Maastricht criteria are basically in place to ensure an adequate level of convergence between
prospective and current members of the EMU. These measures take
into consideration that setting up a union engenders considerable pres-

sures for fiscal transfers and migration flows. The specific provisions of the Maastricht criteria guarantee that participating countries are not excessively heterogeneous. Whereas Maastricht addresses more nominal aspects of convergence; this study concerns itself more with the process of catching-up, i.e. real convergence. This means that the standards of living between current and prospective members of the EMU are progressively growing closer, or converging. However, fulfilling the requirements of Maastricht can imply accepting costs in terms of output gap and unemployment. According to the provisions of the Maastricht criteria, prospective members have to bear the entire burden of these costs of convergence.

Admittance to the EMU seems to be an adhesion contract: If CEECs are not able to surpass the Maastricht qualification thresholds, they are denied access to the EMU. But, by reshaping their exchange-rate policies at the outset of ERM-II membership CEECs lay the foundation for passing considerable costs of convergence on to current EMU-members. Accordingly, the transition phase of ERM II is considered a bargaining game with regard to the (re-)distribution of costs of convergence between prospective and current members of the EMU.[2] A policy of gradual escalation – i.e. brinkmanship – could result in an exchange-rate crisis, thereby undermining public support for European integration within the CEECs. In this respect, prospective EMU-members can force current members to provide pecuniary assistance under specific circumstances. Brinkmanship represents a deterrent threat turning CEECs' run-up to the EMU in a two-stage threat game. Such threatening requires that current EMU-members are willing to pay for CEECs' admittance to the EMU. In this regard, it is presumed that western European governments are interested in the economic and political stabilization of CEE. In this context, the 'EU-enlargement' project is interpreted as a joint investment of both current and prospective members into the (simultaneous) provision of the public good 'political stability' in CEE. The current members' willingness to pay for final completion of the 'EU-enlargement' project – in terms of the CEECs' admission to the EMU – is derived from this rationale. As a consequence CEECs are predisposed to moral-hazard behaviour. Ultimately, if a CEEC can credibly risk political stability, they will elicit the current members'

---

[2] Attaining EMU-membership completes the EU-enlargement process. It is presumed that current members of the EMU would draw on other so-called 'member states with a derogation' – i.e. the non-euroized members of the EU – to bear the respective burden, as well. Thus, the terms 'EU' and 'current members of the EMU' are used synonymously except when otherwise expressively stated.

willingness to pay. A prospective member country's leverage is based on threatening to implement exchange-rate policies that considerably aggravate the probability of provoking an exchange-rate crisis. Such currency crisis is usually associated with voter unrest. The upshot of such strategy is that a CEEC deliberately risk deteriorating political stability by infuriating their own constituency against their government's course towards continued European integration. In this way, a CEEC threatens to jeopardize the entire 'EU-enlargement' project. To put it bluntly, it is shown that the bargaining between prospective and current members of the EMU consists of an exchange that sustains public support for European integration in CEECs for some kind of financial assistance by current members of the EMU. The according stance of exchange-rate policy is denoted as 'threaten-thy-neighbour'. That is, prospective members avail themselves of these detrimental external effects of exchange-rate policy making. The resulting bargaining outcome displays a CEEC's ability to pass a portion of the burden of costs of convergence onto current EMU-members, and both sides' willingness to pay for the provision of the public good 'political stability' in CEE. At the same time, potential setbacks on the CEECs' perilous path toward the EMU are effectively internalized and stabilization is achieved.

The key findings and achievements are as follows: This work is a theoretically guided analysis and orientated towards empirical projections of CEECs' exchange-rate policies with respect to the eastward enlargement of the eurozone. The inquiry aims at detecting potential setbacks in the course of the EMU-enlargement process, and determines the ability of an enlarging EMU to react to such challenges. The deployed political-economic approach is accentuated by a system-theoretic framework, which allows for a consistent and coherent modelling of economic and political decision-making. This modelling also applies to policy-making on the European intergovernmental level, particularly with respect to embarking upon preventive measures, which foster internalizing the external effects of national exchange-rate policy-making. Hence, this work enriches the understanding of theories of European integration. Regarding its contribution to theorizing, the discussion indicates that a political-economic approach may utilize a certain preference concept – i.e. the use of induced preferences. Otherwise, the and coherence of a political-economic approach with regard to behavioural assumptions concerning individual choice would be impaired.

At the heart of this study is the formal modelling and empirical analysis of the adjustment process in the course of eastward enlargement – i.e. the bargaining for costs of convergence within the transition period of ERM II. This investigation results in a game-theoretic analysis of a two-stage threat game comprising the brinkmanship and the study of three alternative bargaining solution concepts – i.e. the Nash-Bargaining, the Kalai-Smorodinsky, and the Ståhl-Rubinstein solution. The game-theoretic analysis identifies potential looming conflicts in the EMU-accession process that have so far not been recognized. The discussion of the various bargaining solution concepts warrants the conclusion that both current and prospective members of the EMU are equally splitting the awarded Maastricht costs of convergence in terms of output gap.

A comprehensive stylized Monte-Carlo simulation of the CEECs' exchange-rate policy choices, in a scenario where all CEECs gain EMU admittance in 2005, indicates that the Baltic countries and Hungary are eligible brinkmanship candidates. Accordingly, these countries may successfully enforce pecuniary claims from current members of the EMU. As inferred by the discussed two-stage threat game, 'new cohesion funds' may be established in 2005, amounting to an estimated 1.7 bn. Euro. These costs correspond to the expenses for an effective internalization of the external effects of exchange-rate policy-making. At the same time, the bargaining outcome reflects both the current and prospective members' actual willingness to pay for completing the European eastward enlargement process, thus, preserving political stability in CEE. This bargaining outcome can be characterized in terms of efficiency and distributive gains. Moreover, the system-theoretic considerations allow for assessing the political-economic formation during ERM II, in terms of the systemic stabilization of the European enlargement process.

This book is structured as follows: Chapter 2 lays the foundation for the subsequent study. Basic scientific ideas for the analysis of exchange-rate policy are outlined. Methodologies of the political economy are reformulated in terms of system-theoretic considerations. The system-theoretic frame of reference also provides guidance for dealing with decision-making in multi-level contexts. In addition, the system-theoretic framework facilitates the organization of relevant political science literature in a convenient way. Economic literature on relevant exchange-rate issues – i.e. in particular currency-crisis models and reviewed. A normative benchmark for judging policy choice in matters surrounding systemic stabilization is derived from the discussion, as well.

After having set the stage for further analysis, Chap. 3 delineates essential features of the eastward enlargement process that differ from previous rounds of enlargement. These constitute crucial junctures that are a prerequisite for subsequent bargaining in ERM II. At the core of this enlargement round is the current members' interest in the admittance of the CEECs, in order to ensure political stability in that region. This encourages the CEECs' moral-hazard behaviour. The crux of the matter is that the Maastricht criteria, such as ERM II, do not constitute effective countermeasures curbing CEECs' moral-hazard behaviour. The entire enlargement process is reformulated as a joint investment project 'EU-enlargement' project leading to the provision of the public good 'political stability'. Furthermore, costs of convergence – stemming from conflicting nominal and real convergence – and costs of default – cropping up in the course of an exchange-rate crisis – are discussed. In essence, the bargaining is a hard bout of haggling over the costs of this investment project.

In Chap. 4, the exchange-rate policies of CEECs are studied in greater detail. To begin with, a brief synopsis of exchange-rate policies in the CEECs serves for drawing a typology of alternative exchange-rate policy stances. Second, peculiarities of ERM II are scrutinized. Finally, political-economic aspects of exchange-rate policies in the CEECs in ERM II – i.e. the facets of "threaten-thy-neighbour" – are studied in greater detail. The discussion in this chapter is the appropriate place to introduce the subsequent game-theoretic analysis.

The game-theoretic analysis in Chap. 5 represents the formal modelling of previous thoughts. The model is basically a two-stage threat game, at which exchange-rate policy is the brinkmanship strategy that constitutes, under identifiable conditions, a deterrent threat. Alternative bargaining-solution concepts are developed and discussed in order to determine in a heuristic manner the most robust equilibrium.

Chapter 6 supplements the analysis in terms of stylized political forecast with empirical projections. Data on costs involved are estimated statistically or taken from related studies. Regarding crucial probabilities of the two-stage threat game, we conduct as an example, a binomial-logit analysis which estimates country-specific probabilities of voter alienation. This voter unrest accounts for changes in attitude towards fulfilling European membership obligations in relation to incurred unemployment during ERM II's pass through. The derived measure approximates the likelihood of triggering a currency crisis in reference to the presumed short-run trade off between employment and the preservation of a fixed exchange-rate regime. Moreover, the empirical analysis drafts current members' remaining influence on decision-making in an EU-25. The estimated probability portrays current members' ability to reject the demand for providing extra fiscal transfers toward CEECs. The Banzhaf-power index is used to calculate this proxy.

The aforementioned parameter estimates are used to make a Monte-Carlo simulation of brinkmanship probabilities in the context of an empirically calibrated two-stage threat game. An advantage of the empirical analysis is that it allows judgements to be made as to which CEECs will likely exercise brinkmanship in a scenario where all CEECs enter ERM II in 2005. The analysis provides an empirical impression for completing eastward enlargement of the eurozone successfully – i.e. retaining systemic stabilization for the adjustment process of European integration. The estimated cost of (maximum)1.7 billion Euro per annum for this process is trifling when compared to a possible destabilization of the public good 'political stability'.

Chapter 7 concludes and assesses bargaining outcomes in light of systemic stabilization. Possible external effects of a CEEC's exchange-rate policy formation in the course of the eurozone's eastward enlargement may heavily disrupt the entire European integration process. The track of the EMU-enlargement process needs to be stabilized politically and voter acceptance of the course must be maintained. Despite the costs involved, effective internalization and successful completion of the European eastward enlargement project remains possible. How these costs are met, whether by raising additional funds among European member states, or by redistributing them within the present framework of social and economic cohesion is a question for future researchers.

2

Setting the Stage

This study concerns the political economy of exchange-rate policies in CEECs. In this chapter, the political economy approach is reinterpreted in system-theoretic terms. In doing so, we aim at expounding a coherent and consistent framework for further research on interdependent decision-making in political and economic systems. This review is conducted along the lines of positivist research. At the same time, we inquire into the (European) multi-level context. By the same token, the normative benchmark 'systemic stabilization' is derived for the argumentation. This measure is well suited for assessing alternative political options in the context of potentially disastrous exchange-rate policies of CEECs in the course of the EMU-enlargement process. In this way, the tool kit for further analysis of exchange-rate policy in European affairs is prepared. With respect to the system-theoretic framework, this chapter concludes by organizing relevant political science and economic literature in order to establish the starting points for our study. This chapter creates a blueprint for the subsequent political-economic analysis of exchange-rate policies during the EMU-enlargement process.

The theoretical framework that is laid out in the following section utilizes methodologies of political economy. The reason for relying on a political-economic approach is due to the our research topic exchange-rate policies of CEECs, which lies at the crossroads of economics and political science. However, mingling two disciplines, which are separated to some extent, requires a coherent and consistent theoretical framework. For this purpose, we structure the analysis with the help of a system-theoretic framework.

2.1 Revisiting Political Economy

The objective of our study is to model the politic-economic aspects of exchange-rate policy making in the course of an enlarging eurozone. It is supposed that political decision-making and economic formation are highly interrelated. This is at the heart of the interdisciplinary research focus of the political economy. The following discussion highlights the compatibility of political and economic decision-making. For heuristic purposes, the political-economic approach is reviewed in terms of system-theoretic considerations.

Political economy treats policy choice as endogenous. Politics is not exogenously provided by some 'social planner' or 'benevolent dictator', but the outcome of a process of political decision-making. This approach comprises more than taking into account the interdependency of decision-making in political and economic systems. According to Drazen [67] such research contrives ways and means of constructing a coherent and consistent methodological approach. The aim is to find equilibrium solutions, at which economic and political outcomes are mutually consistent [162]. For reasons of coherence and consistency, methodologies of rational choice will be applied to the economic as well as political science portions of our study.

A system-theoretic frame of reference facilitates straightforward methodology. Such course of action adds in avoiding redundancies and tautologies. The heuristic value of system-theoretic considerations is in their potential to combine different approaches as well as discriminate between similar ones [114]. However, from the viewpoint of this system-theoretic angle we do not strive for explanation. Rather, we take the advantage of a system-theoretic framework as a modus operandi [133]. In this way, system-theoretic considerations do not setup a theory, because no empirical propositions are intended. It is applied as a conceptual framework in order to indicate and describe the consistency and coherence in theoretical modelling of interdependent political and economic decision-making. The purpose is to sharpen the intuition about the formation of political and economic decision-making. Although, the system-theoretic considerations are restricted to a minimum that is sufficient enough to clarify the shaping of political and economic formation with respect to our study. The system-theoretic underpinning of the political economy serves to enhance the analysis of exchange-rate policies in CEECs in the subsequent sections.

2.1.1 Decision-Making Processes in Societal Systems

The following system-theoretic considerations concern the decision-making processes in societal systems – i.e. the economic and political system. In doing so, we confine ourselves to a necessary minimum of system-theoretic considerations, which are prerequisite to the subsequent analysis of exchange-rate policies in CEECs. We presume that both the economic and the political system are 'isomorphic' – i.e. representing similarity in both form and function. The notion of systemic isomorphism refers back to the work of Deutsch [61]. This section aims at expounding upon this concept – though in a coarse-grained manner – in order to indicate the coherence and consistency of our political-economic analysis of exchange-rate policies in an enlarging EMU.

We begin with the belief that every societal system is 'self-organizing' (see [46] for an overview of this class of system-theoretic approaches). Societal systems such as the political and economic system of a society are marked by a self-organizing principle. The organization determines elements and relations of a system. Relations describe the modes of interaction between elements within a social systems. All social interaction revolves around an exchange of resources and control rights over resources [51].[1] Both the elements and the relations make up the structure of a system. In social systems actors are the elements, whereas – in its most simple definition – institutions are relations. Institutions and relations respectively regulate social interaction. Because elements and relations constitute each other, a system is called self-organizing.

Systems may have an identical organization, though they may differ in structure. With regard to economic and political systems elements and relations are different in each system. However, both are subject to an identical self-organizing principle. According to the self-organizing principle the behaviour of elements on the micro-level shape phenomena on the macro-level. The mediation runs through relations. These direct not only the behaviour of elements from the bottom-up, but also from top-down. In this way the macro-level affects the behaviour of elements on the micro-level, but the macro-level is dependent on the elements at the micro-level because the latter affect macro-level processing.

Given these static axioms, the dynamic ones are as follows: It is presumed that self-organizing systems are open systems as they rely solely on interaction with other systems [42]. Such interactions cause altering

---

[1] In general, Coleman [51] provides the most extensive study on the mapping out of social exchange relations.

states of the system, i.e. either a change in structure or the death of the system [133]. In this context, systems are called autonomous as their permanent change in structure stems from the interplay of internal processes and external stimulations. However, an external stimulus is processed autonomously: External stimulus processing is entirely dependent on the structure of the system. Thus, it follows, that such 'external effects' – as well as interaction with other systems – must be treated recursively [68].

In a similar way, this applies to multi-level systems, as well. Social systems are generally self-organizing systems of n-order as all entities (including individuals) are (sub-)systems. The interplay in a micro-macro context is not only valid in an horizontal view, but also with regard to a vertical orientation such as in multi-level contexts [42]. Feedback from an upper system level to a subsystem is treated as an restriction – i.e. recursive. Despite the resulting permanent change in structure, systems do not fall into decay, but become more complex.

A systemic equilibrium depicts a certain state of the societal system. There is a balance of forces compensating each other at a systemic equilibrium. In the context of a societal system, this means that no tendencies towards change in terms of altering relations, as well as in the behaviour of elements predominate, but the system remains in a state of rest. A societal system can adopt several persisting states. From the system-theoretic perspective it is impossible to determine the superior equilibrium state of a system. Such normative judgement cannot be derived from the self-organizing properties of systems itself. Instead of this, we make use of an exogenously invoked standard of evaluating a system's performance (cf. [134], further [189]). Accordingly, we adhere to a stationary equilibrium model [134]. From positing a certain state of a societal system a necessary path of systemic stabilization can be derived. In contrast, a benchmark 'systemic stability' can be drafted in order to separate it from systemic equilibrium. Holling [112] has coined the term 'resilience'. The latter expresses a system's ability to respond and adapt to external stimuli by reshaping its systemic structure, thereby perpetuating its self-organizing feature.

A problem of system-theoretic frameworks is that they make up a mere taxonomic description of social interaction. However, a foundation of elements' and actors' behaviour respectively in a multi-level system is required. At this stage, the political economy makes use of rational choice: It is assumed that actors behave in a way, which is optimizing their individual utility with regard to their specific calculus given their preferences and constraints. An actor's behaviour is explained by such rationality. This constitutes rational choice as an actor-oriented and preference-founded logic of decision-making. Thus far nothing is said about the actors' calculus, their preferences and constraints, nor how these are shaped within a multi-level system. It can be simply stated that actors make decision in line with the mentioned determinants. Such proposition meets in triviality: All actors make decisions. As long as nothing more can be explained, the epistemological gains are zero [29]. Therefore, a very important part of a rational decision-making theory lies in determining the range of actually available options of alternatives behaviour and in rather specific hypotheses about the underlying ordering of these options [6]. Therefore, it is necessary to expound the structural characteristics for choices, preferences, and constraints. This reasoning coincides exactly with what is called the 'logic of a social situation' [165]. In accordance with this line of argument, we follow Becker [19] supposing that actors maximize their utility in relation to economic and political markets as particular spheres of a societal system. In this way, the micro-macro structures of systems can be reconstructed. At the same time, strategic behaviour of actors in societal systems does not impede that reconstruction as long as the systemic structure shapes these actors' behaviour [79]. The very same is valid in regard to the processing of uncertainty in actors' calculus when this uncertainty relates to a particular instance.[2]

Subsequently, we deploy the system-theoretic blueprint on to the economic and political system. Likewise, we make use of compatible decision-making theory encompassing individual decision-making and collective action, which are fundamentally conceived to reflect identical exchange relations [35]. Both branches of decision-making theory in economics and political science are re-conceptualized. An advantage of this track is to bring both disciplines closer together, and to highlight the coherence and consistency of the political-economic approach. The decision-making processes in economics and politics are both sketched as an interplay of supply and demand of basic units.

2.1.2 Rational Choice in Economic Systems

In this section, actors' behaviour in economic systems as well as the concept of preferences is briefly overviewed. When the concept of preferences is reconsidered in order to make it feasible for analysis of decision-making processes, a closer look at its axioms is inevitable. Although

---

[2] Such circumstances especially appear in context of our analysis of strategic behaviour and the according game-theoretic model in Chap. 5.

it is not intended to provide another textbook treatment, it becomes easier to begin with a survey of the working of the economic system in line with rational choice methodologies.

The emphasis of decision-making processes in economic systems is on actors maximizing their utility given a set of preferences and constraints. Rationality conveys an instrumental logic, in which actors choose an option that serves them best with regard to their subjective perceptions. Relevant system-theoretic elements in economic systems are households, firms, and (scarce) resources usually in terms of factor inputs and private goods subject to consumption and investment. Households are the utility-maximizing individuals in regard to income-spending. Firms are utility- or profit-maximizing entities, as well. Ultimately, the objects of exchange are resources and control of resources. The exchange of factor input serves as a device for gaining claims on the social product. In this regard, money is only a lubricant for exchange. From a system-theoretic point of view, both kinds of elements must maximize their utility. With respect to firms it can be noted as fact that they follow a trial and error procedure when supplying private goods. If they fail, they will not reproduce themselves as elements of the economic system. The central relation in economic systems is the market-price mechanism connecting the formation on the micro- and macro-level. Moreover, there may exist relations that impede a smooth functioning of a market clearing price mechanism. Market regulations can represent such institutions impairing the efficacy of the market-price mechanism. Both market regulations and market-price mechanism represent institutions, which affect the macro-behaviour of economic systems. For the time being, it is enough to envisage (exogenous) institutions as constraints. As studied in North [154], they have an impact on the choices actually available to the actors, on the sequence of their interaction, and on the structure of information [207]. Such constraints act on expectations of both consumers and firms. Accordingly, consequences of choice in terms of demand and supply of factor input and private goods become foreseeable. Hence, institutions are also prerequisites for calculable choices.

The interplay of supply and demand is balanced out at a point of systemic equilibrium. At this point no actor has an incentive to make further exchanges since no external stimuli – i.e. exogenous shocks – are operating. Usually, researchers postulate a particular state of an economic system as desirable. An economic system can adopt several states of equilibrium – ranging from its 'death' to its Pareto-optimal performance, at which no actor's position can be enhanced without making a another worse-off. However, Pareto-inefficient states may also occur, which result from market regulations counteracting the clearing of markets.

In order to eventually obtain testable assertions the concept of preferences, which are depicted by utility functions, must be introduced. The basic assumption is that there exists a preference ordering for alternative options, or simply, consumption bundles that satisfy particular axioms:

- transitivity: This implies that preferences in a sequence of pairwise choices cannot appear to cycle.
- completeness: This axiom means that an actor has a well-defined preference – i.e. reflections upon alternatives have already taken place and the actor makes a meditated choice.

These two assumptions are inevitably required in order describe an actor making consistent comparisons among alternatives.[3] These axioms enable to obtain *rational* preferences. The subsequent axioms make specific limitations to consumers tastes:

- continuity: A mixing of alternative consumption bundles or options is possible. The axiom of continuity guarantees the existence of topologically pleasing 'at least as good as' and 'no better than' preference orderings, and its purpose is primarily a mathematical one.
- convexity: A balanced average of otherwise 'extreme' bundles is preferred. This axiom ensures that there is a unique best option.
- monotonicity: This axiom supposes non-satiation in the demand for available options and consumption bundles respectively.

Together with the two aforementioned assumptions these axioms allow for *well-behaved* or primitive preferences. By assigning utility values rational choices can be calculated – i.e. an empirical assertion can be tested and, hence, positivist requirements can be satisfied.

On the subject of systemic mediation, the following relations and institutions respectively gain particular attention: In regard to 'non-satiation', given that resources are scarce, the actors' budget constraints counteract their needs, which exceed the resource endowment in the economy. The budget constraint ensures on the micro-level that

---

[3] These axioms encompass the reflexivity property – i.e., broadly speaking, the order in the sequence of pairwise choice is irrelevant. Nevertheless, all these properties and axioms are highly debated particularly in context of experimental studies. Note that these discussions are not subject to our study.

an actor's bilateral commitments – in terms of supplying factor input and demanding portions of the produced social product – can be realized. The systemic relation that coordinates and balances out all actors' needs with the existing resource scarcity in the economic system is the market-price mechanism.

For out purposes, the operation of decision-making in economic systems can be easily portrayed. In the following section, we apply the self-organizing principle to the political system. At the same time, we put emphasis on dealing with preferences. In both areas, considerable differences crop up when compared with rational choice in economic systems. For this reason, the subsequent considerations gain more attention. As a conclusion of this discussion, we emphasize that decision-making processes in political systems can be incorporated with decision-making processes in economic systems in a consistent manner.

2.1.3 Rational Choice in Political Systems

In this section, decision-making processes in political systems in reference to rational choice are modelled. In accordance with the self-organizing principle, elements and relations are assigned. In particular, relations that connect the micro-behaviour of elements with the macro-phenomena of a political system become prominent. In addition, the scope of the preference concept in regard to political decision-making is discussed.

The elements of a political system are voters and politicians. The exchange relation is again characterized by supply and demand of respective resources, i.e. policies and public approval. The according interplay of demand and supply can be designed analogously to the economic circulation of factor inputs and goods (see Fig. 2.1). It is immediately evident, that the most striking difference is the lack of a general unit of account, i.e. money as aid in impediments to exchange [51].

This much simplified scheme of the workings of a political market can be described as follows: It is an exchange of policy supply by politicians – in the form of a government – which, in turn, demands public approval by voters. The voters, again, demand policies with which they desire to supply their assent. The role of politicians can be characterized analogously to firms. In particular, incumbent politicians are required to follow a procedure of trial and error with respect to supplying the claimed policies. If they fail to satisfy voter demand by supplying inadequate policies, this results in sorting out politicians as system elements. Political markets equilibrate supply and demand of policies. In regard

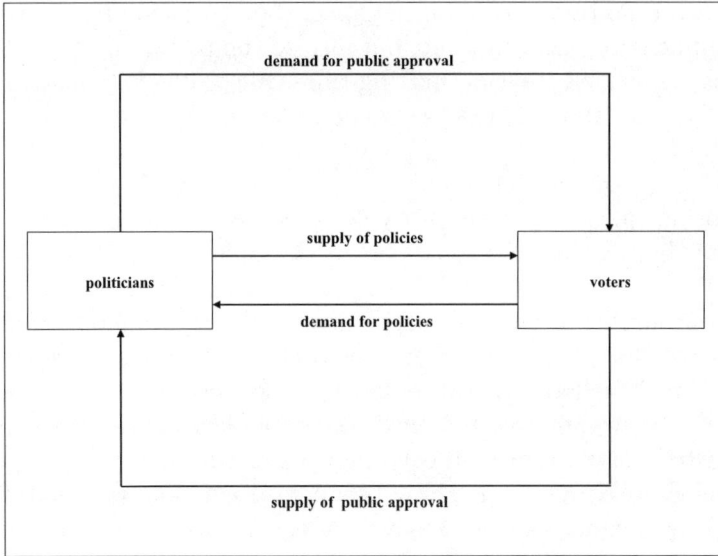

Fig. 2.1. Exchange relation in political systems

to our system-theoretic frame of reference, the balancing of individual demand and public supply carries out analogously to the market-price mechanism. However, a detailed delineation of systemic relations – i.e. the set of institutions, which transform individual preferences for policy demand into a specific policy supply – requires further elaboration.[4] At the heart of political markets is the idea of electoral competition in the tradition of Schumpeter [184]. In this regard, we deal with voters and politicians as individual utility maximizers. Furthermore, politicians, in particular governments, are treated as vote-maximizing entities seeking office-retention [66].

Public approval and policies, which are the resources within the political system, require further comment. For the purpose of our system-theoretic considerations, we imagine and reconcile the provision of public approval with economic factor input in functional terms. In this respect, a once supplied unit of public approval is irretrievably used for the production and supply of a policy. Policies, however, are treated as public goods. Policies are not provided by individuals, but by a public

---

[4] Weidlich [206], for instance, presents a stricter though very comprehensible system-theoretic view on modes of interaction between politicians and voters.

authority. The provision of policies does not necessarily refer to the supply of material resources – for instance, the provision of infrastructure as a public good – at any time, but also to the provision of institutions such as alternative decision-making rules. Accordingly, policies have an impact on the allocation, as well as on the distribution of resources in terms of fixing resource control rights. As is the case with public goods in general, policies are characterized by non-rivalry and non-exclusivity. The former means that several voters can 'consume' the same policy without diminishing its value. The latter implies that all voters are affected by the provision of policy – i.e. a voter is generally not ostracized from 'consuming' a specific public good. Like consumers, voters have preferences for policies. Concepts of preferences, a complicated issue, are outlined in detail in the following discussion within this section. Fortunately, we are able to contribute to a clarification of the impediments to construction of theory in light of the political economy. In particular, we deduce from the subsequent discussion, which preference concept is adequate for our analysis of exchange-rate policies throughout the eurozone's eastward enlargement.

It is assumed in literature that individual preferences for public goods are induced preferences – i.e. they are derived from underlying well-behaved or at least rational preferences [141]. The latter implies that there is a preference ordering of voters over alternative policy supplies that satisfies the requirements of transitivity and completeness (see above). Corresponding utility functions are derived from primitive utility functions defined over composite bundles of private and public goods (such as policies). We strive for treating consumers and voters as only functional differentiations of individual actors in the economic and political system. For reasons of logical consistency, both patterns of decision-making or behaviour should be modelled equivalently.

With respect to consistency, there is a serious complication with induced public sector preference, which may not inherit all properties of the underlying primitive utility function [59]. In this context, it is especially pointed at 'separability', which is a conventional property based on assumptions about specific demands. From 'separability' follows the notion that consumers (voters) prefer a concrete level of public goods (policies). In doing so, they ignore the potential impact of their policy choice on their income prospects and thus, on affordable private goods [141].[5] In this context, only the consumers' (voters') involved tax lia-

---

[5] A thorough discussion of specific properties of separable preferences would consider the role of income and substitution effects in greater detail [62]. Nevertheless,

bility is of particular relevance: In accordance with the completeness axiom, an individual actor considers all feasible options of composite bundles of private and public goods before making choices. The provision of public goods (policies) generally entails costs which are financed via taxes. When demanding a concrete level of policies an individual actor takes the tax burden involved into account. The individual tax liability involved in policy choice affects certainly opportunities for consuming private goods. Therefore, an actor demands a specific level of public goods (policies) – i.e. the single-peakedness of individual preferences for public goods. In reference to such induced public sector preferences, the assumption of separability entails that an individual's most preferred level of any policy is independent of changes in its endowment or wealth. Preferences of this kind are called quasi-linear – i.e. an individual's additional income would entirely be allotted to the consumption of more private goods. In regard to the separability assumption, such preferences imply that voter demands for policies have no impact on their opportunity for consuming private goods. However, the issue of choice is more than complex than simply choosing between two different states of policy supply because this choice affects private consumption possibilities [60]: For instance, if we view civil engineers as actors who vote on public infrastructure construction, we see that they will most likely take into consideration the effects that voting will have on their employment and income prospects [62].[6] On the contrary, quasi-linearity and single-peakedness with respect to the expenditures involved in individual public-sector preferences is commonly assumed in the literature. Despite this imposition on actor behaviour the quasi-concavity of underlying utility functions and thus well-behaved preferences are preserved.

Moreover, there is a restricted domain of Euclidean preferences, which is very popular in political science. This class of preferences imposes even more severe restrictions on public sector preferences. This applies to both the actors behaviour and the quality of public goods concerned. The hallmark of Euclidean preferences can be illustrated in comparison to induced, quasi-linear preferences. In a pairwise comparison between public goods (policies), an actor with induced preferences

---

we confine ourselves to this simplified line of argument as it is sufficient enough to bring out serious problems in dealing with actor preferences in the political economy.

[6] The critique in literature on dismissing the effect of policy choice on prospective income and (future) private consumption is sometimes very outspoken: "In short, many applications of rational choice analysis to politics are either not well-articulated, not fruitful, or both" [141].

considers each policy's impact on its individual budget and its possibility to consume private goods on the basis of the involved tax liability. For this reason, actors always choose a particular level of public goods. Regarding Euclidean preferences, however, one presumes as a rule that voters do not take into account any effect of policy choice on their budget.[7] Euclidean preferences are exogenous instead of induced preferences. Apart from this restriction on voter (consumer) taste, the Euclidean preference concept supposes that policy alternatives are independent of each other – i.e. there is no relative price for two selected policies.[8] Therefore, Euclidean preferences have the disadvantage of placing more restraints on actor behaviour than induced preferences.[9]

The treatment of public-sector preferences for policies, which are in line with well-behaved preferences becomes even more complex, when we consider societal instead of individual preferences. The Arrow impossibility theorem [5] is at the heart of reflections on the aggregation of individual preferences to societal preferences, that do not injure the properties of well-behaved preferences. The latter comes into question because the Arrow impossibility theorem proves that societal preferences violate the transitivity axiom of rational and well-behaved preferences. To be more precise, the only collective choice mechanism in a pairwise comparison that is always transitive is a dictatorship. The fact that societal preferences are not well-behaved does not speak against utilizing any preference concept. Rather, it indicates the relevance of institutions and systemic mediation respectively for explaining the supply of policy.

The discussion of individual public-sector preferences with well-behaved properties generates valuable insights. We have begun commenting on voter preferences with the aim of bringing about a most appropriate preference concept for a comprehensive political-economic analysis. As a result, it has been shown that both quasi-linear and Euclidean preferences impose restrictions on individual actor behaviour. However, the former is a less restricted domain of preferences in terms of individual taste and qualities of public goods (policies). Such in-

---

[7] For the case of an uni-dimensional policy space with 'budget' as the relevant issue Euclidean are akin to quasi-linear preferences.

[8] The rigorism of Euclidean preferences can be relaxed towards non-separable or even convex Euclidean preferences. In such instances, the different salience of policy issues and the mutual dependence of alternative policy issues would be permitted. Notwithstanding, this would leave the according public sector preference exogenous.

[9] Milyo [142] attempts to prove that public-sector preferences are never Euclidean. This puzzle is left to the interested reader.

duced preferences immediately function to account for individuals as both voters and consumers. Euclidean preferences, in turn, are certainly not to be dismissed. It has become clear that Euclidean preferences for policies imply that functionally differentiated individuals as consumers and voters exhibit two different patterns of behaviour. Nevertheless, this class of preferences is appropriate without making concessions in applications of committee voting and related bodies. These models do not tackle individual voters immediately. Therefore, such analyses use models of its own kind.

Our discussion points to the well known story in political science regarding the treatment of voter preferences, which is of relevance to present academic dispute [37]. In order to come to a concluding statement concerning our commitment to a most appropriate concept of public sector preferences, we must briefly overview further objections to well-behaved preferences.

The concept of well-defined voter preferences is of great significance to political science disputes for various reasons. Basically, further caveats can be attributed to the completeness axiom of well-behaved preferences with respect to the so-called 'knowledge problem'. The latter occupies an important place in the abstract thoughts regarding exchange relations in societal systems [35]. Altogether, three objections can be identified. These can be differentiated in representing, first, a rather misleading critique. Second, the completeness axiom is challenged by an alternative research branch. The third objection refers to advantages in terms of the analytical tractability of Euclidean public sector preferences.

According to the completeness axiom, actors such as voters have well-defined preferences. This implies that voters are fully informed about the implications of all offered policies (public goods) – i.e. actors make meditated choices. In spite of this, most often there are policy issues involved that imply a great deal of consequences which are not fully grasped by voters. There may be an individual lack of adequate information. In literature, such a circumstance is described as the 'knowledge problem' [109].

A common cavil is to discredit well-defined preferences by declaring these a "hyper-rationality" [175]. The motivation of this objection is that the completeness axiom is unrealistic because it demands too much actor deliberation. This critique is unsubstantiated in so far as the value of a model does not rest on whether its assumptions are realistic or not. According to positivism, a model's quality depends inter alia on its explanatory range (see above). Secondly, a school of thought in research that also weakens the completeness axiom in connection with the knowledge problem is the constructivism in political science. The constructivist view in political science is closely related to research approaches, which call the construction of exogenous preferences into question [135].[10] Discarding the completeness assumption rather accounts for the starting point of the constructivist critique of rational choice. Constructivists add that the process of deliberation and discourse is of particular relevance when explaining preference formation and decision-making outcomes. Again, the interjection is based on rejecting a model assumption.[11] A third caveat in respect of the knowledge problem calls into question the notion of 'voter sovereignty' and, accordingly, the completeness axiom as well as rational choice. Due to information and transaction costs voters are rarely well-informed about policy implications. Accordingly, it may be seemingly understandable to assume that voters do not completely assess how their alternative policy position choices affect their possibilities for consuming private goods. Therefore, with reference to the knowledge problem, it can be possibly admitted that the application of the Euclidean preference concept may be an estimate for explaining actors' behaviour. Although, this particular objection to the completeness assumption concerns simplifications in empirical analysis, while our previous considerations dealt with issues of theoretical modelling. Euclidean preferences may be an adequate concept – though used with reservation – because there exists no suitable algorithm for reconstructing the impact of alternative policy positions on the private consumption possibilities of an electorate. Accordingly, Euclidean preferences enable approximations in empirical research. Nonetheless, it seems to be rash to discard general objections to the concept of Euclidean preferences just by implying that this preference concept keeps analysis tractable.

In sum, both preference concepts are acceptable when the constituency is not differentiated in its functional forms of voters and consumers because no significant information would be lost. As long as we exclusively account for the decision-making process in political systems, the logical consistency of theoretical modelling is not at stake. However, in regard to the political economy – i.e. examining both the

---

[10] Williamson [212], however, models the formation of actor preferences from the viewpoint of rational choice.

[11] In contrast to the 'hyper-rationality' reproach constructivism opposes rational choice with an alternative modelling of social interaction. Whether and to what extent both research strands are complements or competing approaches is not at the heart of our research study. We resume this question in the subsequent section 2.2.

decision making in political and economic systems – the application of Euclidean preferences obstructs the construction of a coherent and consistent theoretical framework. As a rule for research conduct we suggest to use induced preferences over against Euclidean voter preferences when dealing simultaneously with both voters and consumers. In this way, preferences for policies are modelled in line with the portrayal in the Edgeworth box [198]. The contract curve depicts all feasible allocation of policies, which represent Pareto-optimal equilibrium solutions.

Let us shed some light on the systemic mediation within a political system that acts on the processing of individual voter preferences into societal preferences. The role of institutions representing the systemic relations deserves more attention. Systemic relations in the form of an extensive set of institutions incorporate the micro-behaviour of voters and macro-phenomena. As a result of this, a specific policy outcome is produced. In this regard, the systemic mediation within political systems works analogously to institutions in economic systems, i.e. market regulations and particularly the market-price mechanism. Just as in economic systems institutions constrain the behaviour of relevant actors. This applies, for instance, to voters with regard to expressing their preferences in terms of voting behaviour.[12] In general, such institutions determine in which way voter preferences are aggregated and transformed into policy supply either by way of electoral institutions, legislative rule-making, and/or bureaucratic processes [186]. In this context, a crucial difference to the formation of economic systems becomes evident. Contrary to baseline economics, political systems are especially characterized by a principal-agent relation of voters and politicians. In terms of economic categories, there are only a few suppliers of policies (public goods). The electoral competition is dominated by parties. As is the case with individual politicians within parties, the latter are obliged to win a majority in democratic societies. In accordance with this argument, an incumbent government is required to respond to voter demand in connection with restrictions stemming from institutional constraints within the political system. Policy supply is, therefore, a result of interaction between voters and politicians within an institutional setting. An alteration of the institutional setting can fundamentally affect policy outcomes.

The systemic mediation gives rise to further problems. Again, the Arrow impossibility theorem (see above) occupies an important place:

---

[12] See, for example, the study of Klingemann and Wessels [128] on the impact of different electoral institutions on individual voting behaviour.

It points at setbacks in the process of aggregating individual preferences in terms of infringing the Pareto property. One result of Arrow's impossibility theorem is that the institutional setting and the process of systemic mediation become especially relevant. Politicians are agents assigned to collective decision-making. The politicians face the possibly unpleasant consequences of aggregating their principals' preferences, thereby risking some voter alienation. Closely related to this observation is the work of Buchanan and Tullock [36] and Buchanan [34]. These authors highlight the merits of constitution building – representing a particular set of institutions – protecting a minority against the 'tyranny of the majority'. Generally, beneficiaries in political markets can fully compensate losers for their losses. Such Kaldor-Hicks compensation make recalcitrant losers still better off, thus, embodying Pareto-improvements. However, a minority can also demonstrate predatory ambitions toward the ruling majority. Though, they are unable to readily compensate outvoted majorities [36]. Therefore, politicians bear the consequences of deciding whether and to what extent losers are compensated.

Furthermore, every political system is characterized by a set of institutions, which establish mechanisms of selection in the process of aggregating individual preferences to societal preferences [51]. Moreover, whether specific public sector preferences are enforced also hinges upon the ability of coalitions of voters – i.e. interest groups, citizens' actions groups etc. – to organize their interests as outlined in the seminal work of Olson [158].[13] The specific circumstance of systemic mediation with respect to the principal-agent relation may disrupt a smoothly functioning political system. This relates to the withdrawal of a good deal of public approval. This withdrawal is traced back to voter discontent with the performance of collective decision-making processes. In system-theoretic terms, incidents and outcomes of systemic mediation lead to restructuring, or the death of a political system. This sheds light on the term "decisiveness" [201], which means the capacity of a political system to maintain its ability to act and decide. This describes what we have noted as corresponding with Holling's [112] notion of system resilience above.

---

[13] A general theory of policy formation would have to emphasize the role of interest groups in detail. Yet, this study develops only a minimum of an analytical framework required for dealing with our research question. We assume that the issue of unemployment is of high importance throughout the entire constituency. Therefore, the role of interest groups in policy formation is ignored.

In the context of the systemic mediation, the dominant role of parties – forming agencies or cartels of politicians – in electoral competition is seemingly another objection to our assumption of well-defined preferences. The principal-agent relation turns out to be very challenging for voters in terms of making meditated choices. Because of encountering just a few parties as policy suppliers, voters are required to cast their vote on policy platforms. A voter is unable to combine single components of a party's policy platform. The latter is a composite bundle of any number of policies – i.e. public goods, – to which voters provide their public approval in exchange. In this context, the knowledge problem reappears in terms of information costs: Due to the fact that voters are hardly in a position to survey all aspects of policy platforms they draw on past experiences and performance evaluations of parties. Accordingly, voters behaviour can be grasped in terms of bounded rationality [188]. Thus, voters develop 'party preference profiles' [160]. Voters can certainly collect a host of information to enhance their knowledge. However, the impact of a single vote on the ultimate outcome in electoral competitions is only marginal. Given a cost-benefit calculus of voters, it may be not rational for them to spend much effort on the accumulation of information regarding the supplied policy platforms (see Carling [45] for a thorough discussion of the 'paradox of voting' from the viewpoint of rational choice).[14]

To some extent the process of political decision making itself generates, shapes and transforms individual preferences catalysed by media in the public sphere. In accordance with the knowledge problem and in reference to offering a multiple policy supply, politicians can manipulate the policy supply.[15] By the same token, the constitution – in terms of predetermining the systemic mediation of preferences and as an incomplete contract – also gives politicians considerable leeway and control rights. The reason that principal voters delegate control rights to their agents can be explained in terms of incomplete contracting: Due to the fact that it is impossible to specify all future contingencies implicated in enforcing (aggregated) voter demand, corresponding competencies are delegated to politicians [147]. Therefore, voters cannot fully mon-

---

[14] In addition, public approval does not necessarily need to occur in terms of deliberate voting for a party. In the context of our simple sketch, the notion of 'permissive consensus' [119] of the public provides a sufficient understanding.

[15] The knowledge problem encompasses information and transactions costs. Modelling decision-making processes in this manner allows for explaining the occurrence of electoral cycles. By the same token, there is plenty of room for politicians to manoeuvre in by favouring separate voter or interest groups, which may be of use in securing their reelection.

itor and enforce politicians to redeem their policy promises given in advance to their election [161].

Certainly, both features – the principal-agent relation as well as aspects of the knowledge problem in context of systemic mediation, i.e. the processing of individual voter preferences, – seemingly oppose any arrangement concerning well-defined preferences for policy issues. However, this is primarily a question of research design: As soon as we consider a pivotal policy issue – either in terms of a median voter position in a broad public spectrum or in regard to special interests that have gained political clout, – such assumptions of well-defined preferences can certainly be adopted. Whether politicians confront claims of concentrated voter interests or a demand of the general public hinges upon the research interest and the quality of a particular policy issue.

In general, one can simplify that the decisive systemic relations, which convert all individual voter behaviour – i.e. the micro-behaviour of elements in a political system – is the set of valid political institutions. Individual preferences are processed within these institutions into societal preferences, as a result of which policy outcomes – i.e. macro-phenomena – are generated. Again, no tendencies of change will ensue, if no voters have an incentive to deviate from their initial choice.

Yet, the easiest way to construct a systemic relation that harmonizes micro- and macro-behaviour is to recall that we consider policies as public goods. Due to our approach of modelling voter preferences as induced public sector preferences, we are in the position to re-introduce restrictions in terms of budget constraints in the same functional manner. Particularly, in relying on induced preferences – i.e. linking explicitly policy demand to income – we can step back to the relation 'budget constraint' on the micro-level. When we model the demand for policies that have an impact on voters' and consumers' income via the tax burden involved, then the budget constraint balances voter demand for policies with the (material) resource endowment at a certain period in time.

The system-theoretic considerations concerning the decision-making processes in both societal systems – i.e. the economic and political system – have highlighted the isomorphism we presumed at the beginning. Both spheres of individual decision-making processes can be modelled in an consistent way. The same principle of self-organization has been applied to the economic and to the political system. We have reformulated the political-economic approach in a way that allows for multiple instances, which, however, share the same pattern of behaviour. Every time, we have considered the formation of elements – i.e. the actors involved – and relations – i.e. effective institutions – in terms of systemic mediation linking micro- and macro-level.

By surveying the systemic mediation, differences between the formation in political and economic systems occurred. The most striking difference lies in the principal-agent relation of voters and politicians particularly with respect to the knowledge problem. The differences are limited to the functionally distinguished elements and the institutions in systemic mediation. Market regulations and the market-price mechanism prove to be less complicated compared with the set of institutions, which is effective in political systems. Nevertheless, both systems differ only in their systemic structure and, thereby, in the way they process external stimuli. This way, the political and economic system exhibit an identical systemic organization.

In addition, we have used the system-theoretic perspective as a heuristic device in terms of a conceptual framework. In this manner, we have revealed potential setbacks of deploying different preference concepts in political and economic systems at the same time. The logical consistency of modelling interdependent decision-making in both societal sub-systems can be at stake. This applies particularly to research that analyses political and economic decision-making actors simultaneously. Otherwise, no difficulties will arise if a preference concept is employed in a political science or economic analysis. However, setting up a restricted domain of well-behaved preferences in both economics and politics prevents inconsistent theoretical modelling. Explanations for patterns of behaviour in economic and political systems are derived from the same individual preferences. In doing so, we take advantage of obtaining a single political-economic equilibrium.

Albeit there are potential problems in dealings with preferences and considerable differences in system structures, we can understand and connect economic and political decision-making in a consistent and coherent way. Having reinterpreted the political-economic approach with respect to a system-theoretic frame, both theories of economic and political decision-making can be principally integrated in a unique theoretical approach as is intended in the political-economic research programme.

Our study explicitly conducts an analysis of interdependent political and economic decision-making. Therefore, with respect to the demand for public goods, in particular policies, we refer to quasi-linear utility functions when modelling the decision-making of consumers and voters.

In the following section, we turn to the European multi-level context. Relevant literature in the field of European integration is briefly reviewed and structured along the lines of our system-theoretic framework.

2.2 Refreshing the Analysis of European Integration

We have highlighted that political economy focuses on phenomena that lie at the crossroads of political science and economics such as exchange-rate policy. However, until now we have dealt with the national dimensions. In adding the international dimension, the process of European integration is addressed. This coincides with our elaboration on the system-theoretic multi-level context (see above). In general, this section is an instalment of our system-theoretic considerations on exchange relations. Additionally, pursuing this track facilitates arranging of the relevant literature on European integration and Europeanization issues. Though, we neither intend to deliver a detailed survey of the literature, nor provide an extensive review of alternative methodological approaches dealing with these issues in general. This is an inventory of relevant literature which helps organize the arguments of our study. Additionally, the system-theoretic course taken results in substantiating an alternative standard for assessing European policy-making. This constitutes our benchmark for the later evaluation of exchange-rate policy choice, and the performance of political systems in an enlarging EMU.

The remainder of this section proceeds as follows: At the beginning of our survey, we inquire into the reasons and motivations behind the cooperation of national states. Then, we make our way through recent literature on Europeanization and the European integration process respectively,taking on an actor-centric attitude.[16] It is not intended to analyse this particular literature extensively, but to carry out a tentative systematization of the literature. The purpose is to point out complementary research approaches, which are compatible with the political economy.

In dealing with Europeanization it must be assured – from the angle of a system-theoretically underpinned political-economic –that a macro-phenomenon such as the European integration process is explained by

---

[16] Accordingly, we do not overview the (neo-)functionalist literature which is of no importance to our research approach and topic.

rational choice as well. At the start of discussing the formation of policy choice, in particular with respect to the European multi-level context, is the question of relevant actors as the pivotal elements of the system. From the perspective of an actor-centric approach, most relevant actors are governments, which intermediate between domestic and European or international levels. It must be explained from the viewpoint of a rational actor calculus, why national executives cooperate, and why these national sovereigns gradually delegate decision making – i.e. control rights – to the European level.

At first, there must be a catalyst for engage sovereign states in cooperation. From the system-theoretic viewpoint these are external stimuli stemming from the performance of other – i.e. here national – systems. This applies to economic as well as to political systems. In economic theories of European integration such incidences are called external effects [169]. In this setting, governments are forced to take the transnational spill-over effects of each national policy supply into account [193]. Cooperation stems from efforts to overcome, in particular, negative external effects.

Research referring to the regime-theoretic and to the neo-realistic school of thought focuses on state behaviour. This research strand has been enriched by the institutionalist view in political science.[17] Due to the supposed anarchic environment of international relations, a state must necessarily rely on self-assertion [126]. Broadly speaking, within this environment national executives push for the preferences of their constituency. They do so in order to surmount insufficiencies or external effects of otherwise nationally determined policy supply. In this respect, establishing institutions in international relations can be an advantage.[18] Institutions allow for a convergence of actor expectations in relevant policy fields that are subject to coordination and cooperation [102, 127]. International institutions reduce the costs of obtaining and processing information. Thus, institutions allows for quick decisions and responses to incidences in the context of international relations [163]. Institutions are self-stabilizing, because the effect of suspending an institutions is marked with relatively high uncertainty and a possible reconstruction involves additional costs [193].

---

[17] 'Insitutionalisms' are differentiated in sociological, historical and rational choice institutionalism (see, for further discussion, [7, 106]. We maintain the rational choice approach.

[18] Again, institutions are understood as in North [154] (see above). Sometimes these are denoted as 'regimes', as well. With respect to the system-theoretic frame of references both constitute systemic relations.

Thus far, we have explained why governments campaign for cooperation and why they institutionalize it as well. However, a link between state behaviour and the system-theoretic multi-level context, especially in European matters, must be made. Governments constitute the pivotal elements at the interface between the formation of the national political system, which has been thoroughly described in the foregoing, and the superordinate European level. In this way, the interplay of micro-behaviour and macro-phenomena – i.e. here a policy outcome on the European intergovernmental level – is established. The literature on Europeanization offers a great deal in terms of explaining the formation of such connected system levels. Although, the following approaches take into account the actor-centric view, the chain of causation reducing the trigger of state interaction to one or the other level is rather vague or incoherent [97]. For this reason, rational choice approaches in European integration theories do not constitute a unique theory, but rather a common research programme. Nevertheless, against the background of our system-theoretic framework we point to a possible arrangement of various rational choice approaches.

Basically, two different camps investigating the Europeanization of policy-making can be distinguished (see, for an overview, [39, 214]): In the first camp, there are the 'supranationalists' arguing in favour of the European level considerably influencing the national policy formation. The opposing camp is captured by the 'intergovernmentalists', who favour a bottom-up approach. According to their view, national policy-making shapes the formation of decision-making on the European level in contrast to the supranationalists' obvious top-down notion. These two camps can be reconciled within rational choice. Moreover, there exists a superordinate debate on constructivism and rational choice in European integration theory.[19]

The contemporary state of a common institutional framework on the European level stems from the process of Europeanization. Sandholtz and Zysman [178] – both the most prominent advocates of the supranationalists – argue that the driving forces of the European integration process are political entrepreneurs. This applies in particular to the EU-Commission and European business groups. Moreover, Sandholtz [177] posits that the process of European integration itself alters

---

[19] Pollack [164], for instance, provides an overview of the constructivism versus the rational choice debate in context of the European integration and international relations theory. Keck [124], for instance, points at scopes and limits of the overlapping of both schools of thought. Note that we do not adhere to constructivist approaches (see above).

policy options for actors on the national level in terms of scale and scope – i.e. with regard to forming alliances as well as to opening up new policy fields. The most distinguishing mark of the supranationalist view is that such authors reject the mainly national-state centric view on the European integration process. In a similar vein, prominent advocates of the 'governance' approach – for instance, Kohler-Koch [130] – conjecture that the exclusive focus on state actors, especially with respect to emphasizing the role of European Intergovernmental Conferences (IGC), is of limited research value for a comprehensive understanding of the European multi-level context. According to this view the role of political elites, most notably in the daily practise of European decision-making, is of greater importance.

To the contrary, the intergovernmentalists, Moravcsik [145] – the protagonist of the (liberal) intergovernmentalism camp – emphasizes national executives acting in the European Council and the Council of Ministers as the main actors in the European integration process. In line with Moravcsik's bottom-up view the national preference formation – i.e. the policy demand stemming from the systemic mediation of individual voter preferences particularly interest groups (see with this especially Milner [140] – determines the policy positions of a government in intergovernmental negotiation [146]. The process of European integration is explained accordingly by the dynamic and structural forces embodied in a certain policy field within the domestic arena. Thus, national interests may either bear a retarding moment or work towards further integration [202]. In addition, intergovernmentalists allow explicitly for the European level to effect the formation of policy choice on the domestic level [147].

The general impression is that both camps are rather complementary approaches [214]. Although without the ambition to come to a concluding judgement, our system-theoretic reading of the political economy is of particular help. Actors on the European level can have leeway in influencing the national process of policy formation. In observance of the specific notion of the political economy, this applies, first, when the systemic structure or, more precisely, the institutional rules in decision-making processes on the European level provide for an agenda-setting or gate-keeping role of supranational actors such as the EU-Commission. Second, leeway evolves when the policy issues at stake do not encounter invincible voter or (organized) interest group resistance. This applies particularly to European day-to-day decision making that does not gain political clout in national electorates. Otherwise, as soon as a policy field in European matters gains prominence in a national electorates' opinion, the explanatory stress is on the agent role of governments. Certainly, the above-mentioned leeway arising with respect to the knowledge problem is preserved (see above). It is worth noting, that this mirrors what we have identified as the inevitable recursivity of system-theoretic causality – i.e. the performance of European processes hinges upon the policy formation of the subordinate national systems.

The key to understanding the European integration process is the two-level metaphor of Putnam [167], which was originally referred to the "Schelling-conjecture" [179]. The two-level metaphor postulates that national executives intermediating between the domestic and the international or intergovernmental level have to make allowance for the (national) ratification of any agreed upon intergovernmental decision. This is also valid in regard to our study of the exchange-rate policies in the course of the coming EMU-enlargement. The two-level image has been the subject of various studies, which have elaborated on the interplay of decision-making processes in a vertical perspective – i.e. the mutual dependence of intergovernmental public approval in the domestic arena.

At the heart of the two-level approach is the assumption, that all potential agreements on the intergovernmental level must be ratified in the domestic arena. In this regard, public approval cannot only be traced back to 'divided government' features, such as formal parliamentarian procedures or constitutionally prescribed referenda. It can also be traced to a permissive consensus of voters and lobbies that can enforce substantial political conflict potential [167]. From this argument it follows that governments in intergovernmental negotiations are tied to the formation of policy positions at the national level. Such a domestically constrained executive can make use of its internal 'weakness' in terms of enhancing its bargaining position in intergovernmental negotiations. This is the essence of the Schelling-conjecture. However, such tying-hands strategy may not come to fruition when executives cannot credibly establish such constraints. The problem is that governments may also untie their hands very easily [159]. These vestiges go back to the aforementioned leeway granted politicians to manipulate policy supply – i.e. to modify a multiple policy platform in terms of absorbing specific voter demands, which create compensations for unpleasant European stipulations (see above).

In spite of this, credibility in intergovernmental bargaining can be enhanced by uncertainty – i.e. asymmetric information among bargaining parties – regarding the efficacy of tying-hands strategies. In addition, one actor's threat – most notably, when bolstering the threat by stirring up a crisis – can considerably reshape the bargaining by altering the costs involved (see for comprehensive studies, for example, [181, 183]). However, as is often the case with tying-hands strategies, threats have to be buttressed up. Hence, national executives are required to signal to competing bargainers that backing down is costly. This can be accomplished by creating audience costs – i.e. making promises to voters on the domestic level, while reneging ex post provokes constituencies to rise up against their agents [83].

The time horizon of the negotiators is of relevance, too. In general, bargaining always takes place in the context of simultaneous negotiations in various spheres. The negotiating parties are well aware that they will meet again by some opportunity. Tsebelis [200] puts this into the image 'nested game'. In this context, however, Fearon [82] stresses that intergovernmental negotiators face both a bargaining and an enforcement problem. Given the 'long shadow of the future' in the spirit of 'nested games' one may suggest that a once agreed upon intergovernmental bargain is more likely to be implemented in the domestic arena, as more efforts can be taken towards monitoring and enforcing the agreement. At the same time, however, the long shadow of the future provides plenty of opportunity to renegotiate the terms of the deal – i.e. postponing implementation in hopes of acquiring more favourable terms [84].

Apart from the two-level entanglements, the specific terms within a deal are of interest. Intergovernmental agreements are not necessarily taken by mutual accord or at a lowest common denominator. Similar to national political systems, majorities can make Kaldor-Hicks compensations to outvoted minorities in terms of side payments (see above).[20] In addition, negotiating executives have the ability to initiate issue-linkages allowing for a range of mutually acceptable choices. These can occur either in terms of package deals or log-rollings in European legislation. With this, intergovernmental agreements can be achieved which are beyond a lowest common denominator. Furthermore, states can pool and delegate sovereignty to supranational entities at the European level (such as the ECB and the EU-Commission) [147]. Regarding the majority-minority complex, the same difficulties arise as with respect to the national process of policy formation in the aforementioned. Again, the systemic stability in terms of 'decisiveness' (see p. 24) on

---

[20] In the literature, structural funds, for instance, are often deemed as compensatory payments [26]. We will argue in the same way.

the European level can be contested in the same way. In addition, the efficiency and the distribution of gains are particularly interesting properties of bargaining outcomes relevant to the context of our study [147]. In accordance with the Coase theorem [50], whether or not politicians represented by national executives are able to eliminate the external effects of national policy supply, depends on specific conditions of negotiating with respect to transaction costs involved.

Until today, Europeanization and the process of European integration is characterized by an incremental pooling of sovereign rights. Relevant actors in play are national states, which have voluntarily relinquished their sovereignty to a certain degree. Europeanization is described as a process of increasing reciprocal dependence of decision-making. This goes for horizontal and vertical decision-making processes within and in-between different policies (see [103] for a similar characterization of the European sphere). This process has resulted in establishing a highly interweaved framework for intergovernmental negotiations.

We have argued that current EU-member states have proceeded to cooperate in order to surmount the shortcomings and drawbacks of national policy-making. This applies primarily to the external effects of policy supply such as exchange-rate policy choice. This is the subject matter in the following section.

2.3 Strands of Research in Exchange-Rate Policy

Generally, this section aims at revisiting the political-economic approach. Exchange-rate policy is arranged therein. In what follows, we briefly review the literature on exchange-rate issues in order to lay out the foundation for further analysis of exchange-rate policies in the course of the eastward EMU-enlargement. In addition, the subsequent overview links the policy field exchange rates to the previous discussion on external effects of policy choice. At the same time, references are provided to our system-theoretic framework.

Exchange-rate policy has scarcely been a research topic for political science analysis, but has a tradition in the field of economics. Exceptional political studies are, for instance, Frieden [98] emphasizing the role of interest groups and Aspinwall [8] focusing on the formation of national preferences for the stability of exchange rates in order to explain the origins of the EMS. With regard to the political economy, insulated economic studies comprising systematic data approaches to the relevance of political factors influencing exchange-rate policy choice are covered by Alesina and Wagner [2], Bussière and Mulder [43], and Eichengreen, Rose, and Wyplosz [75]. In reference to exchange rates as a general economic research subject, a great deal of literature has evolved. Broadly speaking, two strands of approaching exchange-rate issues can be distinguished: First, there are the so-called monetary approaches that focus on the long-term balanced exchange rate, such as the Purchasing-Power-Parity theory. Second, there are portfolio-balanced approaches which take notions of risk into account.

With respect to our study, it is quite useful to refer to the exchange rate as an asset price. The external value of a currency is not only reflecting macroeconomic fundamentals and microeconomic risks – for instance, capital market imperfections – but also dependent upon expectations of future economic policies. The asset price definition refers to the strand of portfolio-balanced approaches. The exchange rate is considered here, one of the prices that equilibrate markets for financial assets. Nominal exchange rates behave as asset prices. Changes in its value are due to new information. Potential shifts in political decision-making function as signals. Hence, information alters expectations concerning present and future economic conditions, such as the exchange rate [94, 95]. The asset price definition of exchange rates fits perfectly into our political-economic analysis, because it evidently incorporates economic and political decision-making. Moreover, the asset price view allows a characterization of exchange-rate policy as a public good. That is exchange-rate policy is devoted to the performance of the interplay of specific voter demand and supply by politicians. In addition, by defining the exchange rate as an asset price we can evade the issue of determining the actual equilibrium exchange rates of CEECs. Instead of this, we content ourselves with a tautological definition of an exchange rate to be undervalued if revaluation expectations arise. In turn, an exchange rate is overvalued if future devaluations become predominant [113].

Related to the political-economic understanding of nominal exchange rates in terms of the asset price definition, are studies on the occurrence of currency crises in the context of fixed exchange-rate regimes. Relevant literature distinguishes a first and a second generation of currency-crisis models. First-generation models stem originally from the work of Krugman [131]. According to these models, politicians are myopic and ruin their economic fundamentals open-eyed. In this respect, politicians practise financial or monetary policies that are inconsistent with the preservation of the fixed exchange rate. That is, governments do not consider the costs of a future breakdown of a fixed exchange-rate regime, at all. The second-generation models are traced back to the work of Obstfeld [156] and assume rational actor behaviour. Although, a country's economic policy formation and its fundamentals may be consistent with a particular fixed exchange-rate regime, market sentiments can turn abruptly against them. This argument is derived from making allowance for a governmental loss function encompassing the trade off between short-run employment (respectively output) and the long-run credibility of fixed exchange-rate regimes. The latter is most often gauged by additional points in inflation. This work presumes a short-run stable Phillips-curve in the tradition of Barro and Gordon [17]. The currency-crisis models in spirit of Obstfeld provide for 'multiple equilibria': There is always a certain chance that a government reneges on the exchange-rate promise in an open economic system. As soon as we allow for stochastic or exogenous shocks, there can be a temptation for governments to refrain from their commitment. Instead of adhering to politically uncomfortable states of the economy – for instance, in terms of infuriating voters by aggravating unemployment levels, – politicians may give in to short-run employment and output objectives. Accordingly, speculative attacks test a government's credibility of a given promise to preserve a once determined fixed exchange rate.

Following these strands of exchange-rate crises, the spread of currency crises via contagion has gained more attention in literature. With respect to the system-theoretic reading, contagion represents an external stimulus or effect of national exchange-rate policy formation on to other economic systems. Three channels are distinguished [76]: First, contagion can occur due to real economic linkages in terms of deteriorating other countries' international competitiveness. A change in the nominal exchange rate affects the real exchange rate of a country. Thus, its purchasing power and so, its competitiveness in world markets is determined. The more one country's competitiveness deteriorates in the course of an other country's default, the higher the likelihood of a speculative attack. Second, contagion stems from financial linkages. For example, a shortage of financial liquidity in one country can have dire consequences in terms of triggering a reversal of capital flows in other countries, which are in debt to the defaulting country [3]. Such turmoil in financial markets can have an effect on the stability of the exchange-rate regime.[21] Third, contagion can be traced back

---

[21] See also [123] for a detailed survey of transmission mechanisms turning banking crises into currency crises.

to information asymmetries and uncertainty, which relate to the afore-mentioned knowledge problem. Herd behaviour of economic actors is imagined as follows [89]: Each single investor as a rational actor has some information about the fundamentals, albeit, with a small amount of error reflecting his uncertainty. Being aware of this uncertainty, an investor can never be sure that the fixed exchange rate is ultimately sustainable. Thus, investors try to take into account the possible assessments of other investors, or they are oriented toward similarities of countries. If a critical level of investors – perceiving the fundamentals to be necessarily corrected – is realized, than other investors will likely follow suit. In this regard, the single investor chooses to sell the currency on the assumption that the others have good reason to do so. This is rational behaviour, because of the opportunity costs for obtaining additional information. In addition, profit-maximizing economic actors are in peril of possibly being worse off in case of being left with devalued currency reserves.

Contagion is the channel by which one country's economic formation impedes the other countries' economy. This corresponds to an economic interdependency in a multi-level system. Due to the fact that the performance of the exchange-rate as an asset price also depends upon policy choice, a country's exchange-rate policy formation can demonstrate external effects. From the viewpoint of our system-theoretic relaunch of the political economy, exchange-rate policy represents a specific policy supply. This supply of policy produces external stimuli that constitute the starting point for interaction on the European intergovernmental level. The risk that a CEEC will experience a currency crisis is interpreted here as such an external effect. Whether national executives respond to the impending risk in exchange-rate (policy) formation depends on the mediated preferences of national constituencies, politicians' risk-preferences and time-horizon, and the costs involved. In a word, intergovernmental negotiations and prospects for cooperation hinge upon the subjective perception of the likelihood of negative external effects of exchange-rate policies in the course of the eastward enlargement of the eurozone.

2.4 In Lieu of Results

Thus far, we have sketched the basics of exchange relations in economic and political systems. The purpose has been to sketch a coherent and consistent actor-centric political-economic approach. For that purpose, we have utilized a system-theoretic framework. Consequently, we have come across the disturbing nature of different preference concepts. We have opted in favour of dealing with induced, quasi-linear preferences when analysing the political economy of exchange-rate policy. The review of the multi-level context in terms of the European integration process has defined the field for the analysis of intergovernmental negotiations. In addition, a way of reconciling various approaches to Europeanization has been outlined. By the same token, we have taken a quick look at the basics of exchange-rate policy, which we take as a public good supplied by governments.

The developed framework makes it possible to integrate political and economic variables into a comprehensive political-economic analysis. Accordingly, a model for effective policy coordination in European exchange-rate affairs can now be set up. Possible political-economic equilibrium solutions can be characterized with respect to efficiency and distributive gains as far as intergovernmental bargaining outcomes are concerned. Furthermore, the system-theoretic considerations give us another standard at hand. A possible benchmark is systemic stability – i.e. the resilience or ability of a system to react to external stimuli in a way that preserves its self-organization. In reference to an enlarged EU and EMU respectively, this means that an EMU at 22 – or even 25, when taking into account the potential admittance of Denmark, Sweden, and the United Kingdom – maintains its decisiveness or capability of smooth, functioning, decision-making processes.[22] However, this is far beyond our research scope: This study is limited to reveal potential setbacks in the EMU-enlargement process and the research focus henceforth is on exchange-rate policy. To make it pointed, we investigate whether or not Europe arrives at an enlarged EMU. In this respect, we inquire into the conditions of a systemic stabilization of the EMU-enlargement process, and judge policy choice with regard to its corresponding efficacy.

---

[22] Schneider [182] and also Steunenberg [194], for instance, undertake respective studies.

3

The Core, the Crux, and the Costs Involved

This chapter expounds upon the core of the eastward enlargement. The focus is here on the decisions taken at the IGC Copenhagen 1993. In this regard, we inquire into the peculiarities of the reached agreement of Copenhagen 1993. Secondly, it is here explained why the Maastricht criteria cannot effectively restrain the moral-hazard behaviour, and in particular the brinkmanship stemming from those decisions – this is the crux. Thirdly, we specify the involved costs. At that stage, we survey costs stemming from conflicting nominal and real convergence in context of the Maastricht criteria. By the same token, we consider the costs of possible setbacks in the course of the EMU-enlargement process. The purpose of the following discussion is to substantiate a starting point and a concrete working hypothesis, which pave the way for the later game-theoretic analysis.

3.1 The Core

When analysing the enlargement process of the European Union, it is assumed that it has essentially been driven by political rationale: Both parties – current as well as prospective members of the EU – agreed upon the need to stabilize the region of CEE in view of specific geopolitical concerns and security policy interests.[1] At the beginning of

---

[1] Inotai [120] reviews a mixture of arguments for and against the enlargement process. The author stresses security aspects and the need for political stabilization. In a similar way, Sjursen [191] addresses these ideas. Although, she misses the connection with the fall of the iron curtain (see below). Instead, she pushes the normative perspective ahead: Sharing universal liberal values and norms – thus being in a "liberal community trap" [180] – inevitably entails the offering of admission to the EU-club. Such argumentation henceforth, is no longer tracked.

the 1990s after the fall of the iron curtain political systems in CEECs changed fundamentally. Consequently, they entered a rather uncertain phase. At that time, governments on both sides considered enlarging the EU. In doing so, Western European governments were offering to export an established institutional system to CEECs. Governments in CEECs, in turn, have utilized the accession scenario as an 'institutional anchor' for stabilizing their political, as well as, economic systems. By doing so, CEECs should be admitted to European political systems. Thus, the uncertainty of state-interaction with respect to political decision-making in these countries should be considerably reduced. Relevant literature also argues that political gains are at the core of enlargement [13].[2] At the intergovernmental conference in Copenhagen 1993 both parties arranged the eastward enlargement. In doing so, they have decided to stabilize the region of CEE in the long-term. In line with this rationale the entire enlargement process is denoted hereafter as the 'EU-enlargement' project, resulting in the provision of the public good 'political stability' in CEE. We investigate into the peculiarities of the agreements made in Copenhagen 1993 in the following section.

We argue that the decisions taken at Copenhagen 1993 constitute a Pareto-efficient allocation of the (dividable) public good 'political sta-bility' in CEE. The allocation of this public good is efficient as both parties have agreed upon the appropriate depth, timing and sequenc-ing of integration, resulting in the realization of the enlargement of the eurozone. At the same time, each player prefers that the other bur-dens the entire costs of enlargement. This is generally the key feature of the free-rider problem. In line with this point of view, Copenhagen 1993 constitutes an incomplete contract as the implementation steps could not be fully monitored and enforced (see above). Current, as well as prospective members have been bound by a strictly competitive situation. In such a zero-sum game, both parties have decided simulta-neously how much to contribute to the public good 'political stability'. Each of them has settled the enlargement with the awareness that one may be heavily burdened with most of or even the total costs of the investment. Accordingly, the present value of the agreed upon level of the public good 'political stability' also reflects actors' fear of being entirely charged with future costs. The players have also looked at the minimum payments that they could face. Both players have chosen a level of the public good 'political stability', the costs of which do not

---

[2] Political reasons have also guided previous enlargements of the EU, for instance, the accession of Greece in 1981. This country was considered a young democracy requiring economic and particularly political support [96].

exceed their perceived benefits of its provision. In the following, we portray this train of thought in detail.

The features of the game H serve as a working hypothesis for the later game- and bargaining-theoretic analysis.[3] The game H revolves around the whole – i.e. the 'EU-enlargement' project starting with Copenhagen 1993 and ending with the CEECs' adoption of the euro at the EMU. At a later stage of this study, we only focus on a specific aspect of this project, i.e. basically the phase of ERM II. However, inquiring in the game H allows for certain simplification regarding the game-theoretic analysis of CEECs' passing through ERM II.

We consider basically a two-person game, in which both players of the set $M = \{1, 2\}$ – a single CEEC$_i$ (denoted as player $j = 1$, whereas $i = 1, ..., n$) and the EU-15 (player $j = 2$) – allocate their initial endowment over some level of a private consumption good and a dividable public good.[4] At this point, the public good is 'political stability' in CEE. The initial position at the beginning of the 1990s can be characterized by relatively high uncertainty. The players have found themselves in a situation of incomplete information regarding net costs and benefits of the proposed 'EU-enlargement' project [64]. Therefore, the decisions taken at Copenhagen 1993 represent an incomplete contract. Neither side had precise information about the actual costs involved with alternative strategy combinations and outcomes. The set of feasible strategies for each player j is given by $S_j = [0, 1]$. This is to say, that the players simultaneously choose strategies out of a continuum between completely free-riding ($s_j = 0$) and burdening oneself with full costs ($s_j = 1$) with respect to the provision of the public good 'political stability'. S_j is as an infinite set of mixed strategies.[5] Burdening the entire costs denotes a player's maximum willingness to pay for the provision of the considered public good. Assuming mixed strategies is

---

[3] For the subsequent studies, it is drawn on Binmore [23], Dixit and Skeath [65], and Holler and Illing [110] without further references.

[4] Actually, the number of actors involved – eight CEECs resisting a monolithic EU-15 – is actually higher than the set of players M. We explicitly refrain from considering the prospective EMU-members as a cartel at a later stage of analysis. At this point and for the sake of the argument, all CEECs are treated as a unitary actor. Certainly, the outcome of Copenhagen 1993 is a settling of all these actors' heterogenous interests. However, we do not explain the outcomes of Copenhagen 1993, but consider in retrospect the decisions taken as an equilibrium bargaining outcome. This equilibrium is the starting point of our analysis.

[5] At this point, we make the usual imposition that the infinite strategy set S is non-empty, closed and bounded (i.e. compact), and convex allowing for unique solutions.

an appropriate representation of the strategic uncertainty – i.e. a situation of incomplete information – the players faced at Copenhagen 1993. The outcome is the provision of the public good 'political stability' given that the players' contributions for financing this investment are sufficient. We assume quasi-linear preferences of both players, who represent as it were aggregated voter preferences. The pay-offs are given by the players' utility functions u_j over the level of 'political stability'. Hence, we can ignore any effects of the provision of this public good on prices and consequently on the consumption of private goods (see our discussion in Sect. 2.1.3). Each von-Neumann-Morgenstern utility function u_j is a continuous mapping from S in $\mathbb{R}^+$. The cost of supplying B units of the public good is $C(B)$, where B denotes the (political) benefits of integration. At this point, we assume that $u_j = 0$ if the player j burdens itself with the entire costs $C(B)$ which just offset his benefits B.

Notwithstanding, we finally look for a Nash-equilibrium in mixed strategies, a convenient point of start for examining the game $H = \{M, S, (u_j)_{j \in M}\}$ is to begin with pure strategies. Figure 3.1 depicts the two players alternative choices between 'financing enlargement' and 'free-riding'.

		EU-15	
		financing EU-enlargement	free-riding
CEEC$_i$	financing EU-enlargement	b,b	b,a
	free-riding	a,b	c,c

Fig. 3.1. 2x2 Matrix of the 'EU-enlargement' project

The outcomes of this interactions are as follows: The outcome a denotes realizing the 'EU-enlargement' project without bearing the costs of financing; b means realizing the 'EU-enlargement' project but being stuck with the entire costs of its financing; the outcome c means having indeed no costs. Consequently and most notably, this outcome involves having no 'EU-enlargement' project and thus, no public good 'political stability'. Both players rank $a \succ b \succ c$. Obviously, both players lean toward free-riding. There are two Nash-equilibria for the strategy combination ('financing EU-enlargement', 'free-riding') and vice versa. Hence, no unambiguous solution evolves in this particular game H for the case of pure strategies. In the following section, we therefore put more attention to the mixed extension of this game.

The further analysis of the game H takes place in two steps. At first, we interpret the agreed upon form of the EU-enlargement – i.e. the speed of widening and the quality of Pareto-efficient solution. This reflects the demanded mutually optimal quantity or level of B of the public good 'political stability' in CEE. Second, we look for B^* resulting from the players' mutually best responses – i.e. a Nash equilibrium of the strictly competitive zero-sum game H. These considerations are prerequisites for the subsequent discussion of CEECs' scope for redistributing costs of convergence in the ERM II.

Given that the public good 'political stability' is dividable any Pareto-efficient allocation must maximize the level of the public good in a way that

$$\max_{B \geq 0} \sum_{j=1}^{2} u_j(B) - C(B) \geq 0 \, .$$

The optimal level B^* is then derived from the condition

$$\sum_{j=1}^{2} \frac{\mathrm{d}u_j(B)}{\mathrm{d}B} \leq \frac{\mathrm{d}C(B)}{\mathrm{d}B} \, .$$

This is the standard Samuelson-condition. The according optimal level of the public good is the sum of players' marginal benefits from the public good equal to its marginal costs:

$$\sum_{j=1}^{2} \frac{\mathrm{d}u_j(B^*)}{\mathrm{d}B^*} = \frac{\mathrm{d}C(B^*)}{\mathrm{d}B^*} \, . \tag{3.1}$$

We can specify even more features of the derived willingness to pay for 'political stability' which finally underpin the unique Nash-equilibrium solution for the case of mixed strategies. The so-called maximin-rule is an alternative solution concept. Usually, such course of action does not result in an optimal strategy choice. Nevertheless, this particular solution concept is applicable in instances of high uncertainty. Copenhagen 1993 has been indeed marked by players' high level of uncertainty about the respective other player's pay-off: Neither the entry date for EU-membership, nor the particular costs involved have been clear at the beginning of the 1990s. Whatever agreed upon implementation steps, both players have been well aware that each of them would attempt to reduce its actual burden of the investment costs of the 'EU-enlargement' project. In this respect, the most obvious decision-making rule regarding the contribution to the provision of the public good has been to maximize each player's respective minimum pay-off. In general, the maximin pay-off – i.e. the gain-floor – of player j is given by:

$$\underline{v}_j := \max_{s_j} \in S_j \min_{s_{-j} \in S_{-j}} u_j(s_j, s_{-j}) \ .$$

Due to the zero-sum situation, there is also in reverse a minimax pay-off for a player j, which is the lowest pay-off – i.e. a loss-ceiling – that the other player can force upon player j:

$$\overline{v}_j := \min_{s_{-j} \in S_{-j}} \max_{s_j \in S_j} u_j(s_j, s_{-j}) \ .$$

The more a player j increases his contribution to the public good 'political stability' – i.e. burdens oneself with more costs, – the better off the other player. This applies in general to strictly competitive games. In two-person zero-sum games it is thus valid that:

$$v_j^* := \overline{v}_j = \underline{v}_{-j}$$

This is a so-called saddle point. Choosing mixed strategies enhances each player's gain floor. Because of modelling here the strategic uncertainty in reference to each player choosing a mixed strategy $s_j \in S_j = [0, 1]$ the ultimate solution is then the Nash-equilibrium $v_j^* = (s_1^*, s_2^*)$. The line of argument is as follows: If player j would choose a pure strategy – so to speak, one of the bounds of the above defined continuum – he would receive a pay-off $u_j = 0$. This is due to the fact that player $-j$, knowing in advance that player j chooses 'financing EU-enlargement', resorts to 'free-riding'. In doing so, player j would burden all costs just offsetting the benefits of integration (see Fig. 3.1). Given the antagonistic players' preferences no stable equilibrium can be achieved at all, if each player anticipates that the other one chooses the pure strategy 'free-riding'. However, randomizing of pure strategies here keeps the players from choosing pure strategies. Playing mixed strategies is the easiest way to prevent one's own choice from being guessed and exploited by the other player. This exactly depicts each player's reciprocal uncertainty regarding the respective other player's maximum willingness to invest into the 'EU-enlargement' project. Current as well as prospective members keep each other guessing about their willingness to pay for some level of 'political stability'. In line with this rationale the game H results in a unique Nash-equilibrium for mixed strategies. For this specific case of the mixed extension of a two-person zero sum game, the previous two Nash-equilibria for the case of pure strategies (see Fig. 3.1) do not represent the players' optimal strategies [148].

In line with this rationale, we can assume that the mutual best answers regarding the Pareto-efficient allocation of the public good 'political stability' satisfy the maximin-decision making rule. Therefore,

$$v_j^* := \sum_{j=1}^{2} \frac{du_j(B^*)}{dB^*} = \frac{dC(B^*)}{dB^*} \ . \tag{3.2}$$

The considerations on the Nash-equilibrium coincide with the specifics of the maximin-rule for the case of the mixed extension of the game H. For that reason, v_j^* denotes a stable Nash-equilibrium. In contrast to the players' maximum willingness to pay, the revealed actual willingness to pay is each time a bargaining outcome.

The maximin-rule applies to all phases of investment up to the completion of the 'EU-enlargement' project by introducing the euro as legal tender in CEECs. Both parties get closer to each other step by step. The final phase of investment is that of ERM II, and the according costs of convergence are leftovers for fierce bargaining. Previous investment costs on both sides along the lines of decisions taken at, for example, Copenhagen 1993, Berlin 1999, Nice 2000, and Copenhagen 2002 are sunk costs.[6] This applies to the costs of arranging the incomplete contract, as well as to monitoring and enforcing costs. A good example of these costs is the pre-accession funding via Phare-programmes[7], the Copenhagen criteria, the acquis communautaire, the present Pre-accession Economic Programmes (PEP), or other instruments of multi-

---

[6] See Williams [211] for a survey on the road to membership for CEECs along the lines of intergovernmental conferences.

[7] The Programme of Community aid to the countries of Central and Eastern Europe (Phare) was already launched 1989 in order to facilitate institution building and investment financing in these countries.

lateral surveillance. There is fierce bargaining throughout all the phases of investment into the 'EU-enlargement' project. Both players have a hard bout of haggling over the actual burden at each integration step. In retrospect, every step in integration depicts a Nash-equilibrium.

To many observers the enlargement process fosters a very asymmetric relationship, in which current members have the upper hand. Regardless of this, the sketched rationale of Copenhagen 1993 shows that the arrangements reflect precisely each players' willingness to pay for the realization of the well thought out investment project 'EU enlargement'. For the time being, the enlargement process is not an adhesion contract, but every player has started from a level playing field in intergovernmental bargaining. The decisions taken at Copenhagen 1993 are assumed to be a Pareto-efficient allocation of the public good 'political stability' (3.1). At the same time, Copenhagen 1993 constitutes a Nash-equilibrium for mixed strategies. Coinciding with the maximin-solution (3.2) underpins the stability of the Nash-equilibrium solution. The core of the contemporary enlargement process is that some candidate countries have presented an application for joining the EU-club. However, the 'ins' are not less interested in the 'EU-enlargement' project. Knowing in advance that the incumbents are willing to provide CEECs with access to their club is a starting position for moral-hazard behaviour. In addition, we have identified that each player's willingness to pay equals his perceived benefits of the 'EU-enlargement' project at each integration step. Accordingly, every investment step reflects a process of moving gradually closer together in a piecemeal way. In this manner, free-riding behaviour is ruled out to a great extent. No one cheats the other. This is a very useful conclusion for the later game-theoretic analysis in Chap. 5. At that point, it is shown what both current and prospective EMU-members are actually willing to pay for ensuring the 'political stability' of CEE in the long-run.

We now come to the crux of the enlargement process. Specific characteristics are explored which encourage free-riding and moral-hazard behaviour respectively. In this context, we inquire into the effectiveness of Maastricht criteria.

3.2 The Crux

The crux of the enlargement process is derived from the political rationale of actors involved: In particular, western European governments have agreed upon the need to stabilize the region of CEE, in view of their specific geopolitical concerns and security policy interests. CEECs know in advance that the EU-15 is thus willing to engage in the provision of 'political stability' and, thereby willing to pay for the EU-enlargement. Moreover, the arrangements of Copenhagen 1993 constitute an incomplete contract, because neither side is able to fully monitor the other's fulfilment of obligations taken under the contract (see above). Moral-hazard behaviour of CEECs is also provoked on account of these circumstances. In the following, we study the moral-hazard behaviour of CEECs in greater detail in order to introduce the fundamentals of the brinkmanship. The focus here is on features of incomplete contracts, and whether Maastricht criteria curb incentives for moral-hazard behaviour.

Presently, after having set-up the 'euro-club', the incumbents want some outsiders to join them. Neither the present EMU, nor a fortiori an enlarged EMU represent an 'Optimum Currency Area' (OCA). Nevertheless, the eurozone may be shaped in that way [58, 92]. Although, in their run-up to the EMU the founding members of the EMU have established Maastricht criteria in the form of a tying-hands strategy in order to force themselves to ensure monetary and fiscal stability in the joint currency area, and to ensure an appropriate operation of the euro [107, 209].[8] The Maastricht criteria are considered to be indicators of adequate convergence. The basic idea is that an applicant state pursuing economic policies in accordance with economic formation of the 'ins' is capable of adapting to a single monetary policy. The nominal convergence criteria of Maastricht comprise the following items:

- An inflation rate of no more than 1.5% greater than the average of the three best performing member states, i.e. with the lowest inflation rate.
- Long-term interest rates must fluctuate within 2% of the average bond yields of the three best performing countries.
- The government gross debt should not exceed 60% of Gross Domestic Product (GDP).
- The budget deficit should be no more than 3% GDP.
- National exchange-rates should remain within a +/- 15% oscillation band around a fixed central parity vis-á-vis the euro for two years preceding the aspired admission to the EMU.

---

[8] Certainly, there has also been some scope for moral hazard, particularly for countries, which may have been considered as rather indispensable to constructing the EMU. In the case of the most divergent southern EU-members, Maastricht criteria have been quite effective forms of discipline. Greece did not qualify as a founding member of the EMU in 1999, but joined later in 2001.

Particularly the exchange-rate, the budget, as well as the inflation criterion are of particular interest in the context of our study. Maastricht criteria shall help to ensure that CEECs stabilize their economies. It is expected that these criteria prove demanding for all CEECs [101].

The crux is that contrary to the time of 1995–97 these Maastricht criteria do not provide a sophisticated tying-hands strategy for EMU-founders, thereby assuring a smooth, functioning EMU: While Greece, for example, as a potential founding member failed to qualify for the EMU for the time being, the political stability of that country has not been at stake. At that time, Greece may have been considered an adequately consolidated democracy not requiring further European economic and political support. Yet, quite the contrary can be assumed with respect to CEECs. The political process and its outcomes are more uncertain when compared with the present formation in current EMU-member countries.[9] At this point, however, some observers may argue that CEECs are already institutionally embedded in European designs of political systems. This is certainly true. Though, retracting concession would jeopardize all CEECs' efforts of preparing for EU- and EMU-membership respectively. In such an instance, their integration into western European political systems will probably be stopped or even reversed. Either way, we consider this option to be politically riskier than following the "pacta sunt servanda" rule, i.e. actually integrating CEECs into the EU.

The reader may object this consideration, because Bulgaria and Romania do not belong to the first wave of CEECs joining the EU in 2004. Obviously, their exclusion has not spoiled the entire enlargement process. This is due to the fact, that when these countries were 'disqualified' both could not comply effectively with Copenhagen criteria. At the same time, most notably, they neither experienced a currency crisis, nor have they been critical actors in any decision-making process within the governance structure of the EU. Accordingly, what the EU-15 actually did, was to keep Bulgaria and Romania successfully at a distance. In this way, the EU avoided potential setbacks for the entire enlargement process by keeping these countries from an inimical rush to join the EU. However, the CEECs of the first wave have successfully qualified for EU-membership and are already committed to the EU. Most notably, the following applies to the CEECs: When they

---

[9] The still apparently high level of electoral volatility in CEECs can serve as an indicator of political uncertainty. There is a vast literature of studies on the volatility of the electorate in selected CEECs. See Birch [24] for a brief survey on that issue.

enter the EU and ERM II respectively, the altered institutional setting
– for instance, their influence over EU policies as well as their access to
transfer payments – will give them plenty of opportunities for evasive
action.

Notwithstanding, Wallner [205] and Burkart [41] argue that CEECs
have no leeway at all during their run-up to the EU and the EMU
respectively. These authors refer to an incomplete contract model, as
well. They also start from assuming that after having fixed an agreement – which is here Copenhagen 1993 – some players' actions cannot
effectively be monitored. This allows for hidden action – i.e. moral-
hazard behaviour – of CEECs in terms of deliberately abstaining from
implementing policies that are in accordance with Maastricht criteria.
Their line of argument is as follows: In course of the adoption of the
acquis communautaire, CEECs implement rules that impair their economic growth [13]. The obliged entry conditions for EU-membership are
specific investments. These investments render current and prospective
members' interactions a hold-up problem. Accordingly, the EU-15 can
impose additional costs on CEECs.[10] The specific investments would
rule out any incentives for CEECs to practise moral hazard by making exit options considerably dearer. It is the effect of rendering specific investments otherwise to sunk costs that dissuades CEECs from
moral hazard. Wallner [205] concludes that the hold-up problem reduces CEECs' – here, most notably economic – benefits from EU-
membership.

The problem of his argument is that he can hardly explain why
CEECs have negotiated exceptions from the acquis communautaire, at
all. Furthermore, it is not obvious that CEECs have made such specific
investments which would become sunk costs, if the 'EU-enlargement'
project will lose momentum, be stalled, or even entirely fail. We can
consider the adoption of the acquis communautaire just as much as
technology and productivity enhancing investments which improve
CEECs' position in the world market in the long-run.[11] Moreover, we
can even interpret the enlargement process as a commitment to economic reforms. In this respect, governments in CEECs act as strate-

---

[10] Although these authors refer in particular to the process of adopting the acquis
communautaire, their argument also applies to the, here considered, costs of convergence. See Brücker, Schröder, and Weise [33] for another view on negotiation
processes during CEECs' reform to the acquis communautaire.

[11] By the same token, we can certainly not exclude the possibility that there are
indeed specific investments in some sectors. An analysis of particular interest
group behaviour casts some light on such details. However, this is not a subject
matter of this study.

gically constrained internal actors, who cannot prevent implementing short-term unpopular reforms, which are quasi stipulated on the intergovernmental level.[12]

The general problem of focusing on economic benefits of the 'EU enlargement' project is the difficulty of attributing economic gains to a player's action. We are, at first glance, unable to decide whether it is the EU-15 that allows CEECs to adopt well-established economic standards and thus, to reduce country-specific risk premia in the long-run. Alternatively, we cannot observe whether it is CEECs credibly committing to economic reform by using the 'EU-enlargement' project as an 'institutional anchor'. With regard to sovereign states as the key actors in international relations we attribute economic gains to CEECs' activities.[13] In addition, the EU-15 cannot effectively keep countries from imitating their economic standards. Therefore, we argue that economic benefits accrue just en passant in the course of a successful adoption of 'western' economic standards. The only issue that can solely be realized jointly is 'political stability' in terms of an effective reduction of uncertainty within both parties' relations. Because of this 'jointness'-feature we argue in favour of moral-hazard behaviour in light of incomplete contracts, and discard alternative considerations regarding specific investments.

This discussion has stated that there is considerable scope for moral-hazard behaviour when passing through the Maastricht qualification process including ERM II. The according moral-hazard behaviour can be traced back to the free-rider problem in general, and is particularly due to incomplete contracting. The crux is that Maastricht criteria do not effectively limit moral hazard.

3.3 The Costs

In the previous sections we have investigated the core and crux of enlargement ensuing moral-hazard behaviour, which here is treated as brinkmanship. When discussing brinkmanship we have to clarify the

---

[12] If the according measures are too unpopular – i.e. infuriating the constituency – then a government may maintain its commitment to and amending their policy-supply (see the discussion in Sect. 2.2).

[13] From the system-theoretic point of view (see Sect. 2.1.3), these economic reforms are ultimately the result of voters' processing of such an external stimulus. The policy supply of market-oriented economic reforms stems thus from voters' effective demand.

involved costs, i.e. costs of convergence and costs of default. The costs are the subject matter of this section.

The disputed costs of the final phase of enlargement are costs of convergence. According to the rationale of Maastricht these costs are charged entirely to a prospective member's account. The costs of convergence stem from possible trade-offs between nominal convergence criteria and real convergence processes.[14]

The narrowing of productivity and price level differentials which comes along with a catch-up in per capita GDP is denoted as real convergence. Driving forces behind real convergence are the liberalization and opening of markets – i.e. allowing for free international trade – as found in the Heckscher-Ohlin-Samuelson model: Countries tend to export goods that use their relatively-abundant factor intensively, which allows for the evening out of differences in relative factor prices across current and prospective member countries in the long-term [25]. Going beyond the neoclassical view on the relevance of factor endowment, the new growth theory says, broadly speaking, that copying technology [18] and deliberate efforts – of firms as well as governments – to invest in human capital accumulation spur real convergence [170]. Overall, openness to international trade, intensified competition, and the realization of comparative advantages by specialization foster productivity and economic growth in CEECs. Although, higher productivity rates in new member countries come along with increasing income levels, i.e. increasing rates of wages. The rising level of wages, however, is not exclusively restricted to the sector of tradable goods: The price level in the sector of non-tradable goods will also increase. Due to a lacking of progress in productivity in that sector, the higher costs on the supply-side – i.e. rising wages – are passed on to author is well-aware that the degree of wage pressure hinges upon the formation of wage-bargaining systems. This discussion is omitted here for reasons of simplicity. While the inflation rates of the CEECs in the sector of tradable goods adapt to the respective level in the current EU due to competition, it is not necessarily valid for the development of the price level within the sector of non-tradable goods. Therefore, a mark-up in prices for non-tradable goods and non-substitutable services in CEECs contributes to an increase in the average price level. Accordingly, countries with higher growth rates exhibit generally higher inflation rates. Such phenomenon has been explained by Balassa [11] and Samuelson [176], and is dubbed

---

[14] See Gáspár [99] for a survey on the interdependencies of nominal and real convergence. Note that we do not discuss issues of Maastricht criteria in great detail, but in context of their impact on growth, i.e. output and employment.

the Balassa-Samuelson (BS-)effect. Adjustments of relative prices during processes of real convergence are generally marked by the BS-effect. This also applies to the CEECs in transition [70].[15]

The Maastricht nominal convergence criteria can impair real convergence processes. First, the inflation criterion can be obviously precarious: Given the BS-effect, deflation in the tradable-sector can be necessary in order to achieve compliance with this particular Maastricht criterion [190]. Meeting the inflation target can come at costs of economic growth and result in output gap – i.e. a fall in actual output relative to potential output. The harsher disinflation policies are, the higher the according 'sacrifice ratio' is. Second, there is a consensus that high public deficits harm long-term growth [187]. A decline in public gross debt may decrease nominal and real interest rates via falling inflation. When meeting the budget deficit criterion, however, fiscal consolidation may require a reduction in public investments, for instance, in infrastructure which may be a prerequisite for private investment and growth. By the same token, deliberate efforts of governments to invest in education, promoting human capital accumulation, are reduced (see above). Third, the formation of the exchange rate is very crucial with respect to the stabilization of capital flows, particularly when combined with inadequate domestic savings and non-mature domestic capital markets [21]. Therefore, prescribed fixed exchange-rates in ERM II are intended to stabilize capital flows by settling down private agents expectations. High volatility of exchange rates would not only impede the stability of the capital influx, but negatively affect growth performance of extremely small open economies such as the Baltic countries. The effect runs through the impact of volatile exchange rates on inflation via the prices of tradable goods, and thus on potential output in the medium term [77]. At the same time, the Maastricht ERM II criterion may prove demanding: When misalignments render the prescribed soft pegs unsustainable, economic growth founded on capital influx is doomed to fail.

---

[15] See, for instance, De Broeck and Sløk [57] for empirical evidence of the Balassa-Samuelson hypothesis in CEECs. In addition to the inflationary bias in CEECs on account of the BS-effect, other channels for inflation are discussed. First, nominal inertia can be expected to continue as long as price liberalization in these transformation countries has not been completed. Until enhanced competition will reduce price dynamics, higher inflation will be the consequence. Second, transition economies have a higher potential for quality improvements than mature markets. Corresponding higher prices are hard to distinguish from nominal increases. Thus, the measured average inflation rates may be higher for statistical reasons [88].

Summarily, meeting the Maastricht criteria can come at the expense
of additional unemployment and output gap. Whether these costs of
convergence in the course of conflicting nominal and real convergence in
CEECs really crop up is a difficult empirical question, which we address
in Chap. 6. These costs are originally burdened entirely by prospective
members. However, CEECs' brinkmanship makes these costs a subject
matter for redistribution.

The brinkmanship is based on possibly provoking costs of default. This
brinkmanship means deliberately threatening to create a currency crisis deteriorating the investment project 'EU-enlargement' and thus the
public good 'political stability'. CEECs can – under certain conditions
which we determine in Chap. 5 – threaten to trigger speculative attacks
on their fixed exchange-rate regimes in ERM II. The preceding performance of fixed exchange-rate arrangements – for instance, during the
former crises in 1992/93 of the EMS, and during the Asian crisis in the
late 1990s 1990s – indicates the vulnerability of soft pegs. Generally,
such come along with a considerable loss in terms of output and employment which we denote as costs of default. These costs have to be
paid by current members, as well. This is due to the fact that the new
members have rather direct access to European structural funds. More
transfers to CEECs may be necessary in order to reassure infuriated
voters who might retract their approval to the completion of the 'EU-
enlargement' project (see Aghion and Blanchard [1] for a discussion on
the 'optimal speed of transition'). In such situations, the entire project
may be at stake. Additionally, current members will probably be faced
with the problem of needing to buy CEECs governments' consent for
some kind of an agreement in European intergovernmental bargaining.
Ultimately, it may be necessary to provide CEECs financial assistance
just to preserving systemic stabilization in terms of smooth, functioning intergovernmental politics within the European institutional framework.

Although currency crises in CEECs would not appear automatically – for instance, due to sizable interventions by the rising need to
raise interest rates would eventually trigger an abandonment of the
exchange-rate regime. This applies all the more so as higher interest
rates would bring about the risk of precipitating a banking crisis, and a
subsequent drain of capital inflows.[16] The latter is crucial for CEECs,

---

[16] Normally, banking crises emerge at the onset of a recession. This holds in particular, if the recession follows a preceding economic activity that was fuelled by
credits, capital inflows, and accompanied by an overvalued exchange-rate [31].

because of the eminent importance to stabilize (net-) capital inflows [54]. A reversal of such capital flows could deteriorate overall economic activity, thus causing a devaluation of a CEECs' exchange rate [91]. Moreover, one country's fall may trigger further speculative attacks. Contagion (see p. 36) usually spreads among countries with similar economic fundamentals and political features as with CEECs [21]. A spreading currency crisis would confront current EMU-members with severe economic and political problems. However, this is an incidence – in line with the above-mentioned rationale of European integration – which the EU wants to avoid. Therefore, knowing that the 'ins' are willing to pay for their accession, CEECs could make use of the implicit risk of loosing public support for European integration – which would spoil the investment project 'EU enlargement', and the according provision of the public good 'political stability' – by putting the exchange-rate regime deliberately at risk. According to the logic of the two-level metaphor, such crisis-bargaining bolsters CEECs' position in intergovernmental negotiations on transfer payments or similar compensations. In this regard the Schelling conjecture means the less voters are inclined towards European matters and thus, the stronger they respond to aggravating unemployment rates, the higher the CEECs leverage in bargaining (see Sect. 2.2). For that reason, CEECs can dispose of an effective brinkmanship strategy – i.e. a deterrent threat enabling to elicit the EU's willingness to pay for political stability. The threat relies on provoking an exchange-rate crisis scenario that entails considerable costs of default. The costs of default usually exceed the costs of convergence, which would be a disadvantage to current members, as well.

In sum, we consider the entire eastward enlargement process as an investment project for ensuring political stability in CEE. The 'EU enlargement' project acts as a key for achieving political stability. However, political stability is a public good, at which both CEECs and the EU-15 are the investors competing for sharing the costs of investment. The core of the 'EU-enlargement' project is that both sides have agreed upon the Pareto-efficient level of the public good 'political stability'. CEECs are well aware of the EU-15's willingness to pay for the provision of the public good 'political stability', inviting them to moral hazard. The crux of the 'EU-enlargement' project is that Maastricht criteria do not provide effective constraints in this respect when non-compliance with Maastricht entails a breakdown of the entire enlargement process. CEECs can effectively put political stability at stake when they have been admitted to the EU. This becomes especially evident if they immediately cause an exchange-rate crisis at the onset of their EU-membership. This holds even in case of adopting an attitude of 'wait and see' regarding the entrance to the ERM II – though, certainly only for fixed exchange-rate regimes. A currency crisis is most likely to undermine the CEECs' aspiration to EMU-membership and public support for European integration in general. Thus, the completion of the 'EU-enlargement'-project and, hence, the public good 'political stability' in CEE is at risk. Accordingly, the policies and public goods which are subject for intergovernmental negotiations are the exchange-rate policies in CEECs. These countries will be provided with pecuniary assistance allowing these governments to cushion their constituency against the hardship of Maastricht criteria.

This chapter has detailed our working hypothesis and the starting point of the game-theoretic analysis in Chap. 5 respectively: The present process of eastward enlargement is marked by the game H. This game incorporates the Samuelson condition as well as the maximin-rule. By the same token, the decisions taken at Copenhagen 1993 have been linked to a set of mixed strategies representing features of incomplete contracting. The crux is that the subsequent moral-hazard behaviour of CEECs cannot be effectively cut by Maastricht criteria. The latter entail the costs of convergence. These are the remaining costs of the investment project 'EU-enlargement'. New members – i.e. governing politicians, always tempted to lessen voter resistance – shrink from taking on these costs. Instead, governments in CEECs attempt to redistribute the very same by practising brinkmanship. Before we ultimately turn to the formal game-theoretic analysis of the brinkmanship, foundations of exchange-rate policies are surveyed. We also explore in greater detail crucial junctures and particular transmission mechanisms of the brinkmanship strategy in the context of ERM II.

4

Exchange-Rate Policies in CEECs

This chapter casts more light on CEECs' ability to pass costs of convergence on to current members of the EMU. The aim is to scrutinize the transmission mechanisms and the range of the brinkmanship. Having already outlined the starting points for an exchange-rate policy analysis in Sect. 2.3, we will first provide a brief overview of the exchange-rate policies in CEECs from the beginning of the 1990s until today. In this context, we also address the issue of trend real appreciation. The latter turns out to be an ancillary condition which renders exchange-rate policies highly sensitive and, hence, an effective instrument for the brinkmanship. Second, we must inquire into governance aspects of ERM II – i.e. the mediation of various national executives' preferences for exchange-rate policy choice on the European intergovernmental level. We will see that there are no effective countermeasures against CEECs' moral-hazard behaviour during their scheduled passing through ERM II. This conclusion is attributed to the lack of institutional precautions in ERM II, and due to particular features of European governance. By examining the endogenous formation of exchange-rate policy – i.e. its provision as a public good – it is demonstrated, third, that the original moral-hazard problem – due to the 'core' and the 'crux' – becomes even more alarming.

This mode of action reveals the national interests of both current and particularly prospective members of the EMU regarding their respective policy choices in ERM II. Being equipped with a thorough political-economic understanding of CEECs' exchange-rate policy making in ERM II – which we then denote as a "threaten-thy-neighbour"-policy – we then analyse it in a formal game-theoretic setting in Chap. 5.

In Sect. 2.3 we set the basics for the analysis of exchange-rate policy – i.e. the asset-price definition and the issues of contagion in the context of seminal currency-crisis models. With respect to these considerations exchange-rate policy comprises two aspects: First, the choice of a specific arrangement and – in reference to fixed exchange rates – the reference currency, central rate and fluctuation band. The second aspect reflects that exchange-rate policy is well influenced particularly by the fiscal and monetary policy decision-making.[1] Ideally, exchange-rate policy corresponds and fits into an optimal policy mix, which would achieve simultaneous internal and external balance. The former aims at price stability and full employment, whereas the latter means to achieve a current account position that is in line with sustainable foreign debt and domestic growth considerations. However, in reference to the typically presumed short-run stable Phillips-curve, inflation and output are conflicting objectives. Obviously, exchange-rate arrangements are not chosen once and for all, but are a reflection of certain economic conditions at a specific point in time. exchange-rate arrangements reflect main alternative focuses of exchange-rate policies: coping with exogenous shocks and transnational policy spill-overs, bringing down inflation, stabilizing real exchange rates, sustaining the balance of payments equilibrium, dealing with large and volatile capital flows etc.

Principally, two ideal types of exchange-rate arrangements with reference to the above-mentioned trade-off can be distinguished.[2] First, exchange-rate policy may aim at pushing the output goal ahead. This is to say that exchange-rate policy would be conducted in terms of a 'beggar-thy-neighbour'-policy – i.e. striving for undervalued exchange rates even up to competitive devaluations. An improvement of external competitiveness – output and employment – would be achieved at the expense of other countries in terms of exporting unemployment. Second, exchange-rate policy can be a subordinate feature of a comprehensive monetary policy aiming at price stability. Both ideal types stretch out a continuum of specific exchange-rate policies. Previous stances of the very same as well as prospective exchange-rate policies of CEECs in ERM II can be classified in this respect.

---

[1] Certainly, other policies such as wage policy and policies concerning social and welfare regimes affect the exchange rate, as well. However, we confine ourselves to fiscal and monetary matters.

[2] When exchange-rate policies are considered hereafter, it only refers to fixed exchange-rate regimes. References to floats are explicitly made.

4.1 Brief Synopsis of Exchange-Rate Policies in CEECs

At the beginning of the 1990s CEECs' economies faced a choice between two different types of exchange-rate policy. They could have selected from a range of alternative exchange-rate policies that lie in between the continuum of the two ideal types: a 'beggar-thy-neighbour'-policy and an exchange-rate policy subordinate to a comprehensive monetary policy of price stabilization. A specific problem of economies in CEECs at the end of the Cold War and after the breakdown of the Council for Mutual Economic Assistance (CMEA) was the complete restructuring of aggregate demand. Openness to international trade gives countries the opportunity to import a price structure similar to foreign producers. When fixing the exchange rate, internal inflation cannot increase too much without loosing competitiveness against foreign producers. Local suppliers react to this pressure partly by reducing inflation, and partly by reducing output as less productive units are pushed out of the market [115]. For this reason, 'beggar-thy-neighbour'-policy has not been a reasonable opportunity to develop external competitiveness and employment. Moreover, a relatively undervalued central parity would have hampered the transition in terms of reconstructing the capital stock [137].

At the onset of the transitional phase, it has been necessary to get rid of the inherited money glut. CEECs had to cope with inflation-ary pressure arising not only from the aforementioned BS-effect (see Sect. 3.3), but also from structural reforms such as price liberalization, dismantling of trading monopolies, removal of trade controls etc. [53]. Therefore, CEECs have been especially concerned with inflation goals. An applicable disinflation strategy can generally be based on either exchange-rate targeting or explicit inflation targeting. Such a disinfla-tion strategy requires specific institutional arrangements (central bank independence, accountability of policies, transparency etc.) to be ef-fective [144]. Exchange-rate stabilization programmes come into con-sideration when both monetary institutions are lacking credibility, and the economy is strongly integrated into the world market. No credi-ble monetary institutions existed in CEECs at the beginning of the 1990s. Therefore, exchange-rate targeting in order to import monetary credibility, thereby providing a nominal anchor for domestic prices has been necessary [93, 100]. With the exception of Slovakia and Slovenia all CEECs performed fixed exchange-rate regimes at the beginning of transition (see Fig. 4.1).[3]

---

[3] This modified figure originally refers to [54].

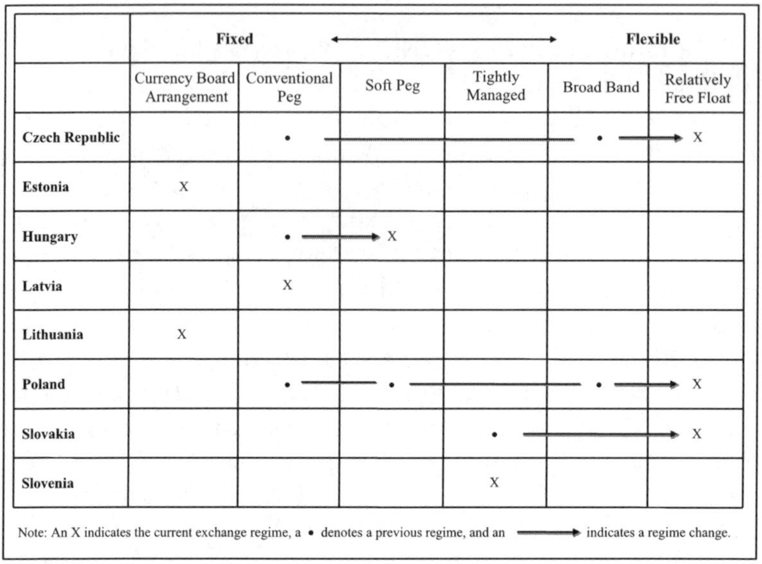

	Fixed ⟵————————⟶ Flexible					
	Currency Board Arrangement	Conventional Peg	Soft Peg	Tightly Managed	Broad Band	Relatively Free Float
Czech Republic		•	·····························—		• —⟶	X
Estonia	X					
Hungary		• —⟶	X			
Latvia		X				
Lithuania	X					
Poland		• ——	• ———		• —⟶	X
Slovakia				• ——————⟶		X
Slovenia				X		

Note: An X indicates the current exchange regime, a • denotes a previous regime, and an ——⟶ indicates a regime change.

Fig. 4.1. Exchange-rate regime changes in CEECs before their EU-accession

In view of the fact that the average inflation rate in CEECs declined from 22.7% in 1995 to 10.5% three years later in 1997, shows that such disinflation strategies performed properly (see table 4.1).[4]

Table 4.1. Inflation trends in CEECs from 1995–2004

	1995	1996	1997	1998	1999	2000	2001	2002	2003	2004
Czech Republic	9,1	8,8	8,4	10,7	2,1	3,9	4,7	1,8	0,1	2,6
Estonia	29,0	23,4	10,6	8,2	3,3	4,0	5,8	3,6	1,1	3,0
Hungary	28,2	23,6	18,3	14,2	10,0	9,8	9,2	5,3	4,7	6,2
Latvia	25,0	17,6	8,4	4,7	2,4	2,7	2,5	1,8	2,9	3,2
Lithuania	39,6	24,6	8,9	5,1	0,8	1,0	1,3	0,3	-1,2	0,2
Poland	27,2	19,9	14,9	11,6	7,3	10,1	5,5	1,9	0,7	2,4
Slovakia	9,9	5,8	6,1	6,7	10,6	12,0	7,3	3,3	8,6	7,1
Slovenia	13,5	9,9	8,4	8,0	6,1	8,9	8,4	7,5	5,6	4,8
Tot Avg	**22,7**	**16,7**	**10,5**	**8,7**	**5,3**	**6,6**	**5,6**	**3,2**	**2,8**	**3,7**

[4] Data source: DB Research (CPI yoy [aop]).

From 1998 onwards average inflation in CEECs has fallen to moderate level around 3% – within in a range of an estimated 0.2% inflation in Lithuania to an estimated 7.1% in Slovakia – in 2004. Although, in particular bigger economies – such as the Czech Republic in 1997, Hungary in 1998, and Poland in 1999 – switched their disinflation strategy from exchange-rate to explicit inflation targeting, which coincided with a switch towards more flexible exchange-rate arrangements (see Fig. 4.1). This provided an alternative signal to local economies in CEECs, showing that stabilization efforts are not over, but are making these more explicit and similar to economies of current EMU-members [115]. In addition, it is well-known that increasing capital mobility and fixed exchange rates render CEECs' economies vulnerable to speculative attacks. This holds true particularly for non-mature markets characterized by non-established and uncertain economic policy patterns [105]. Accordingly, the trend towards more flexible arrangements has been a response to the gradual lifting of capital controls thereby, reducing the risk of currency crises. However, extremely small open economies, such as the Baltic countries, still resort to the use of very tight commitments (see Fig. 4.1) – for the reasons we discussed earlier (see p. 52).

Another phenomenon that has emerged within the 1990s is a trend towards real appreciation of currencies in CEECs. The issue of overvalued real exchange-rates in CEECs has been addressed in context of the BS-effect. However, with respect to the financing of catching-up and the rebuilding of the capital stock a general trend towards real exchange-rate appreciations seems desirable. This desirability is dual-edged in that it is beneficial in terms of the catching-up process, yet dangerous in terms of stabilizing fixed exchange-rate regimes.

The replacement of capital stock and the process of real convergence requires capital influx. Current account deficits balance these capital account surpluses. Higher real interest rates reflect that expected rates of return – reflecting increasing productivity growth – in CEECs are higher than, for instance, in current EMU-member countries. Thus, capital flow ensues. In this context, Lipschitz et al. [132] discern a policy-dilemma: On the one hand, interest rates reflecting real capital scarcity in the prospective member countries would be relatively higher than in mature economies. On the other hand, considerably lower real interest rates would cause an imbalance between domestic saving and investment, causing a current account deficit financed via (foreign) capital [21]. Table 4.2 portrays the trend real appreciation in CEECs.[5]

Table 4.2. Trend real appreciation in CEECs from 1995–2004

	1995	1996	1997	1998	1999	2000	2001	2002	2003	2004
Czech Rep.	34,0	34,3	38,2	35,2	36,0	36,3	35,5	31,2	32,2	30,6
1994=1	0,98	0,99	1,10	1,02	1,04	1,05	1,03	0,90	0,93	0,88
Estonia	15,1	15,5	15,8	15,6	15,6	15,6	15,6	15,6	15,6	15,6
1994=1	0,99	1,01	1,03	1,02	1,02	1,02	1,02	1,02	1,02	1,02
Hungary	181,6	204,8	223,9	253,7	254,4	265,0	247,3	236,1	264,7	245,8
1994=1	1,34	1,51	1,65	1,87	1,87	1,95	1,82	1,74	1,95	1,81
Latvia	0,7	0,7	0,7	0,7	0,6	0,6	0,6	0,6	0,7	0,7
1994=1	1,00	1,00	1,00	1,00	0,86	0,86	0,86	0,86	1,00	1,00
Lithuania	5,4	5,0	4,4	4,7	4,0	3,6	3,6	3,5	3,5	3,5
1994=1	1,08	1,00	0,88	0,94	0,80	0,72	0,72	0,70	0,70	0,70
Poland	3,18	3,43	3,72	3,91	4,23	4,01	3,67	3,85	4,40	4,53
1994=1	1,17	1,27	1,37	1,44	1,56	1,48	1,35	1,42	1,62	1,67
Slovakia	38,4	38,4	38,0	39,6	44,1	42,5	43,3	42,7	41,5	40,0
1994=1	1,01	1,01	1,00	1,04	1,16	1,12	1,14	1,13	1,09	1,06
Slovenia	160,20	175,5	186,8	188,6	197,0	210,9	221,1	230,0	236,5	239,0
1994=1	1,03	1,13	1,20	1,22	1,27	1,36	1,42	1,48	1,52	1,54

It is obvious to see that there is a trend real appreciation in CEECs. Though, overvaluation is particularly evident in relatively big economies such as Hungary and Poland. The Baltic countries seem to be especially successful in stabilizing their exchange-rate (see also Rahn [168] on the issue of trend real appreciation in CEECs). This trend real appreciation and corresponding capital inflows will prevail for other reasons, as well: It can be expected that risk premia in CEECs decline over the course of their continuing integration into EU. By the same token, as the remaining restrictions in the capital account are completely lifted capital flows to CEECs are fostered. In this instance, the composition of capital inflows regarding their maturity structure is of specific interest. While inflows of foreign direct investments (FDI) are rather long-term capital flows, portfolio investments are much more volatile. Moreover, capital flows can be expected to relocate to some

---

[5] Data (in EUR eop) are taken from DB Research. The calculations of the real effective exchange rate (REER) in Table 4.2 are as follows: Each of a single CEEC's nominal exchange rates vis-á-vis other major currencies is deflated by the price indices of the CEEC and the respective country. In this way, the real exchange rates are obtained.

extent from FDI-bearing privatization – which are almost completed in CEECs – to much more fluid portfolio investments [78].

Regarding the performance of interest rates, it can also be argued that only long-term interest rates decline considerably. Nominal interest rates may remain high and aggravate trend real appreciation. This can be due to a convergence play, when prospective EMU-membership reduces long-term fundamentals, but short-term interest rates decline only gradually, reflecting political-economic risks resulting in high risk premia. Relatively persistent, high nominal interest rates would attract even more volatile capital flows amplifying CEECs' default risk [99]. In general, capital inflows may have a positive impact on the institutional building of financial markets in CEECs. At the same time, however, applicant countries are going to be more exposed to sudden, large shifts in capital flows deteriorating the exchange-rate regime. Provided that an overvalued exchange rate does not slow down overall economic activity, further capital inflows increase the risk of exceptional exchange-rate devaluations. The proclivity toward currency crises intensifies in instances where an institutional lag vis-á-vis mature financial markets is present because such inadequacies probably result in bubble-economics. The persisting current account deficits will exert considerable pressure on fixed exchange-rates in CEECs [52].

The problematic nature aggravates, if economic agents adopt to moral-hazard behaviour. A common moral hazard phenomenon is, for instance, the private sector taking ever more substantial open positions [91, 73]. Such behaviour can be due to a perceived implicit bail-out promise. Economic agents may consider CEECs to be 'too-important-to-fail', for example, because of the particular political rationale of the EU-enlargement project (see Sect. 3.1). This holds true all the more so, as a defaulting CEEC may have considerable repercussions on the political-economic formation of other countries [30]. In addition, excessive capital inflows and thus, overvalued exchange rates can have the advantage of relatively cheaper imports. This will probably lead to economic agents' revision of the net present value of their incomes in CEECs and, therefore, to higher consumption [172]. The latter adds to trend real appreciation impairing the stability of the exchange-rate regime. Naturally, we can also make the assumption that consumers anticipate the trend real appreciation and raise their savings quota at the expense of consumption. Even if we presume that households appropriately assess the economic environment, the collective-action problem will reappear – while my neighbour's consumption reduction is always acceptable. Therefore, economic agents' behaviour most probably increases trend real appreciation.

The progressive liberalization of capital flows in the context of the acquis communautaire does not stop the trend real appreciation, but makes the specific exchange-rate policies even more sensitive [116, 143]. Another problem in this context is that current account deficits over the course of real exchange rate appreciations may be considered as an indicator of a impending currency crisis. Although, a large trade deficit can also be the result of increasing confidence in economic policy formation [138]. Generally trend real appreciation can be perceived as an equilibrium appreciation due to significant increases in productivity growth, or as a misalignment indicating a loss of competitiveness. For private agents such effects may be hard to distinguish in specific cases. This gives rise to 'multiple equilibria' (see Sect. 2.3) in terms of a complete revaluation of a present economic situation.

The overall impression is that CEECs aiming at price stability successfully sought to restructure and stabilize their economies. Governments in CEECs resorted to exchange-rate policy as a subordinate feature of a comprehensive monetary policy designed properly to cope with inflation objectives. The observable trend real appreciation is a typical characteristic of catching-up processes. At the same time, overvalued exchange-rates are perils of convergence processes as trend real appreciation and volatile capital flows amplify CEECs' susceptibility to currency crises.

Until now, CEECs have not aimed at undervalued real exchange rates – i.e. emphasizing employment and output goals – in terms of a 'beggar-thy-neighbour'-policy. On the contrary, their currencies have been rather overvalued. The observable trend real appreciation can be conducive to CEECs' brinkmanship – i.e. to threaten to trigger a disordered devaluation. In the following section, institutional provisions of ERM II which may forestall such moral-hazard behaviour are discussed.

4.2 Governance Aspects of ERM II

The main challenge for CEECs has been and still is to make the strategy of entering the EMU compatible with their economic and political necessities. The policy mix required for achieving compliance with Maastricht criteria for membership in the EMU, is likely to slow down output activity and employment (see Sect. 3.3).[6] The focus is on strategic aspects of exchange-rate policies such as the brinkmanship of CEECs when passing through the phase of ERM II.[7] Clarifying the scope of institutional constraints to CEECs' moral-hazard behaviour reveals the depth of the brinkmanship. For this reason, we will now investigate the governance structure of exchange-rate policy affairs in the ERM II.

CEECs lose to a considerable degree their monetary sovereignty after their admittance to the EU. At that time, exchange rate issues become a matter of common concern according to Article 124 (ex Article 109m) of the Treaty establishing the European Community. ERM II, effective since 1999, differs only slightly from its preceding Exchange Rate Mechanism (ERM) in the European Monetary System (EMS). According to the schedule, the process of passing through ERM II will most likely take 27 months. Taking into consideration that entering ERM II takes some additional preparative time to determine central parities and bands, January 2007 seems a plausible estimation on acquiring EMU-membership. The basics of the institutional design of ERM II are shortly delineated in the following paragraph.

The most striking difference in comparison to the former EMS is the 'hubs and spokes'-system: Central parities are only defined vis-á-vis the euro and not against all other participating countries' currencies. Hence, their currencies can fluctuate considerably more against each other, thereby making intervention probably less frequent. Interventions on the margins are binding. However, the Resolution [80] ranks the price stability objective of central banks higher than obligations of intervention. There is also the possibility of intra-marginal interventions on the basis of mutual agreement. The standard fluctuation band is $+/-$ 15% around the central rate similar to the EMS. According to the Resolution, decisions on central parities and the band are taken by mutual accord of the eurozone ministers, the ECB and the minister and central bank governor of a respective member country intending to participate in ERM II. The European Commission and the Economic and Financial Committee (EFC)[8] are only consulted within this procedure. While we can simply assume that the ECB and cen-

---

[6] In this context, related academic literature usually begins by comparing the advantages and disadvantages of alternative exchange-rate arrangements for a CEEC in the run-up to the EMU [185]. However, dealing with these issues in detail would result in losing the thread of our subject of analysis.

[7] Fölsz [90] and Fidrmuc [87] are recent examples in literature taking into account such strategic aspects.

[8] The EFC comprises two representatives of each the European Commission, the ECB, and the current EMU-member countries. It is an advisory board submitting

tral bank governors are generally guided by price-stability objectives, the other decision makers may strive for entirely different goals. The prospective EMU-member country and the ministers of the eurozone – i.e. the 'eurogroup', or, an ECOFIN without the 'members with a derogation' – act as a forum for intergovernmental bargaining allowing for political compromise in terms of issue-linkages, side-payments etc. For that reason the resulting outcome regarding the determination of central parities in the ERM II will most probably fall short of economic first-best solutions in terms of efficiency.

The current members' position regarding the exchange-rate policy choice of CEECs is further detailed: The legal provisions of ERM II allow, for the time being, only a few alternative exchange-rate regimes. Essentially, ERM II prescribes to adopt fixed regimes in the form of soft pegs (cf. Fig. 4.1). The ECB does not actually accept currency boards as a substitute for participation in ERM II [71].[9] Currency boards would offer prospective member countries an opportunity to draw directly on the ECB credit facilities thereby, possibly impairing the ECB's price stability objective. Moreover, the ECB refuses unilateral euroization as an eligible exchange-rate regime when passing through ERM II phase. Due to ambiguous institutional changes within the decision-making process of the ECB, the price stability of the euro may be at stake. This is especially true when market sentiments expect the ECB to be inclined towards CEECs' concerns and possibly accepting higher inflation in the periphery, thus, forfeiting credibility [12]. Moreover, an early accession and consequently too much heterogeneity inside the EMU could complicate controlling monetary policy [69]. Current EMU-members' reluctance to allow CEECs immediate admission to the EMU may also be reasonable because, for instance, the transmission mechanisms of monetary policy and the functioning of automatic stabilizers in CEECs are still unclear. Therefore, they may associate the risks of a premature inclusion of CEECs with a future mark-up on the euro's risk premium. In this respect, the ERM II can be regarded as a measure to continue testing the operation of automatic stabilizers and channels of monetary policy in prospective member countries. Additionally, the Council of Ministers would have no influence over determining the final conversion rates at which the prospective member

---

opinions to and contributing to the work of the Council of Ministers (ECOFIN) and the European Commission.

[9] However, countries that are currently operating with a currency board – for instance, Estonia and Lithuania – may not necessarily be required to float their currency within ERM II before they re-peg it to the euro later (ibid.).

countries enter the eurozone [38]. Therefore, current members object premature admittance of CEECs to the EMU. In particular, the 'ins' oppose unilateral euroization in CEECs during their transition to the EMU, since CEECs would the pass considerable economic risks onto current members.

Decisions concerning ERM II and exchange-rate issues in general are taken within this specific realm of European governance. This applies to intended realignments as well as to potential countermeasures against the brinkmanship. CEECs can also articulate and carry out their particular interests in the context of the specific structures of European governance. Initially, at the request of a prospective member the above-mentioned parties can agree on narrower fluctuation bands than the standard one – as is the case with Denmark running presently a fluctuation band of $+/-$ 2,25% margins. Interestingly and in contrast to the provisions of the former EMS, all parties have the right to initiate a confidential procedure if central rates are deemed to be realigned. Ideally, this procedure allows for the reconsideration of central rates before they deviate too much from real equilibrium exchange rates, making currency crises inevitable. Although realignments in terms of devaluation would infringe on the provisions of the Treaty establishing the European Community, revaluations of central parities are compatible with ERM II (Article 121, ex Article 109j).

Secondly, within the set of the concerned European decision-making bodies countermeasures regarding the choice of the width of oscillation bands and of central parities can be deliberated on. With respect to the choice of bands, the obvious thing to do is to put forth the greatest possible extent of fluctuations bands. This would alleviate the CEECs' default risk. Such broad bands would counteract the negative impact of trend real appreciation on the stability of exchange-rate regimes. However, even such broad bands may be not sufficient to prevent speculative attacks: In January 2003 speculators attempted to drive the Hungarian Forint (soft peg with a $+/-$ 15% band) above its upper limit and thus, triggering a revaluation of its central parity. Although the Hungarian speculative attack was stalled, the occurrence of an attack points to the fragility of even such broad bands. In May 2003 the pendulum swung back: The central bank could not get a grip on excess inflation stemming from the run on the forint during the previous crisis in January. Therefore, devaluation expectations rose and the central bank was forced to devalue the forint's central parity to the euro at the beginning of June 2003. Additionally, despite the fact that exchange-rate policy is a matter of common concern prior to ERM II,

CEECs can introduce smaller bands before entering ERM II. A subsequent widening of the fluctuation bands, though, may signal that both parties cannot agree on an appropriate exchange-rate regime. Accordingly, market sentiments may shift and cause a destabilizing process to ensue(see Bofinger [27] for a more detailed discussion).

With respect to trend real appreciation and crisis-prone soft pegs, (slightly) undervalued central parities seem to be an appropriate countermeasure. This is also valid with exogenous shocks, and in particular positive supply shocks [9, 125].[10] However, the determination of an appropriate exchange rate is a delicate issue (see our discussion on measuring trend real appreciation in the foregoing). A related measure can be a final devaluation before entering ERM II as is the case with the Greek drachma, which devalued by 13 % [52]. Although, it is doubtful that CEECs opt for devaluation, if they can in instances of default possibly rely on the assistance of the EU-15, i.e. pass costs on to current members of the EMU. Apart from central parities and fluctuation bands the timing of entrance to ERM II may be another subject matter of potential countermeasures. Nevertheless, CEECs being sovereign countries can as 'members with a derogation' opt for a crisis-prone fixed exchange-rate regime – outside any jurisdiction of European decision-making bodies.

In summary, there are no institutional constraints within the governance structure of exchange-rate policy affairs in ERM II to curb CEECs' moral-hazard behaviour. There are no effective countermeasures that enable current members of the EMU to keep new members in check; unless, the 'ins' can set up issue-linkages allowing for specific political compromises – such as noticeable devaluations of CEECs' real exchange rates at the dawn of the ERM II. Otherwise, CEECs decide upon their preferred exchange-rate regime. They can affect their currency values in a way which serves their national interest before negotiating admittance to ERM II. CEECs have the upper hand as they can prepare for and implement those exchange-rate policies which improve their negotiating position prior to ERM II. In addition, they can even as 'members with a derogation' deploy a crisis-prone fixed

---

[10] Generally, from an economic point of view, equilibrium exchange rates would be most favourable. They would neither distort purchasing powers, competitiveness, nor contribute to a redistribution of wealth, i.e. no effects on stocks of debts and claims. Yet it must be added, that undervalued central parities favour agents accounting for debts denominated in domestic currency, but make agents who have obligations denominated in foreign currency worse off. The opposite is true in the case of overvalued central parities [56].

exchange-rate regime. It will be seen from what follows why especially soft pegs are conducive to policy-makers' interests in CEECs.

4.3 Political Economy of Exchange-Rate Policy

The remainder of the discussion in this section takes aims to identify the impact of soft pegs on incentives for political agents. The focus is on moral-hazard behaviour of governments in CEECs – which stretches beyond the aforementioned 'core' and 'crux'. The political economy perspective clearly demonstrates that exchange-rate policies of CEECs – immediately after their admittance to the EU – are on a perilous track caused by endogenous policy formation. When addressing exchange-rate policy fiscal policy issues are especially considered. In this context, we also resolve the issue of why governments in CEECs – apart from the EU-15 and the ECB – are reluctant to resort to unilateral euroization.

The prevailing thinking in academic literature considers exchange-rate regimes predominantly in terms of a disciplining constraint [208]. Nevertheless, it is sometimes conceded that governments may be unable to comply with the necessary requirements for maintaining the fixed exchange-rate regime because they encounter political constraints [43]. Setting the priorities for the shaping of incentive structures casts light on the working of exchange-rate policy formation. This is to say, that it is dealt with policy formation as endogenous [210]. In doing so, the moral-hazard behaviour considered here can be grasped. Regarding the political economy of exchange-rate policy, it is assumed that policy-makers are generally vote maximizing. Thus, governments seek to utilize economic policy-making in order to correspond to voters' preferences, i.e. to warrant public approval (see Chap. 2). In addition, it is assumed that policy-makers are actors who greatly discount prospective future costs due to short time horizons. Furthermore, with respect to CEECs it is plausible to take for granted that the electorate in CEECs mostly favours lower unemployment (cf. footnote 13 on p. 24). We attribute this to their individual preferences having been formed in times of socialistic schemes of full employment.

At the heart of exchange-rate stability in ERM II lies fiscal policy, respectively financial policies [104]. According to a simple Mundell-Fleming model, monetary policy is irrelevant and only fiscal policy can affect output and the current account when exchange rates are fixed and capital mobility is high. Soft pegging turns exchange-rate policy into a perilous tightrope act as deviations from a sustainable fiscal policy stance may result in exchange-rate distress (see Sect. 2.3). With regard to CEECs, a most striking example of currency crises occurred in the Czech Republic 1997 [20] and in Hungary 2003 (see above).

From the perspective of political economy, it is difficult for governments – in case of fixed exchange-rates like the soft and adjustable pegs considered here – to implement and maintain a tight policy mix [107]. If there is an output gap and a corresponding level of unemployment in CEECs, then – given particularly downward inflexibility of wages – there may be a voter demand for more (public) expenditure. On the one hand, fiscal policy may need to dampen the social effects of resource movement mostly from the agricultural sector to the rising manufacturing and services sector in CEECs. On the other hand, particularly in case of a 'weak' government, there may be pivotal electorates or interest groups which effectively elicit sizable transfers (see the discussion in Sect. 2.1.3). The case of Spain presents an illustrative example of this: Spain joined the EMS with an overvalued exchange rate in 1989. It experienced a recession and failed to fight inflation effectively. Thus, it devalued in 1992, and anew in 1993 and 1995. Spain experienced considerable capital inflows particularly during the years of 1989–1992. These were due to, first, expected higher rates of return, second, financial liberalization and, third, a restrictive monetary policy and expansionary fiscal policy, which translated into high interest rates. The corresponding real exchange rate appreciation is also imputed to a BS-effect. Most meaningful in this context seems to be the specific role of wages: During the two years prior to Spain's participation in the former ERM, real wages increased moderately and did not developed significantly different from other European countries. However, after the Spanish accession both real and nominal wages rose sharply [10].[11] In addition, loosening a fiscal austerity policy usually provokes a twin-deficit situation. Albeit, relaxed fiscal spending may be comfortable for policy makers seeking reelection. In this regard, rising budget deficits lead to rising interest rates. Higher interest rates ensue more capital inflows contributing further to overvalued exchange rates. The overvaluation of domestic currencies deteriorates export activities and aggravates current account deficits. If governments in CEECs cannot for whatever reasons put implement a fiscal retrenchment, they will aggravate trend real appreciation and bring about a currency crisis. This

---

[11] It is argued in the literature that governments try to buy wage restraint by slackening the reins of fiscal policy [44]. Obviously, such strategy failed in Spain. However, note that the role of wage policies would carry us off the field of investigation without strengthening the scientific insights. At this point, it is only intended to point to another strand of discussion which could later be integrated into our subsequent game-theoretic analysis.

is all the more true as considerable current account deficits, as with CEECs, require a reduction in consumptive expenditure of government budget, perhaps even budget surpluses. Natalucci and Ravenna [152] indicate that such a welfare-inferior policy would probably not be implemented if CEECs' eventual accession could not be credibly denied by the incumbents, which fits our initial considerations on 'the core' (see Sect. 3.1).

Most notably, however, the political incentives generated by pegged rates often fail to provide sufficient fiscal restraints to avoid possible currency crises. This is due to the fact that exchange-rate pegging gives front loaded benefits and delayed costs. Fiscal laxity would undermine a peg only after some time, forcing a discrete devaluation in the future. In contrast to fixed exchange rates, budget deficits lead to an immediate depreciation in the case of floats. Therefore, assuming that the time horizon of politicians is sufficiently short, a government may be tempted to conduct fiscal laxity [199, 129]. Moreover, it is generally high capital mobility which fuels the consequential moral hazard even more. In providing lower cost financing, it may amplify the incentive to lose sight of a prudent fiscal policy, thus, reducing short-run discipline [4].[12] When exchange-rate policy affects private citizens' welfare and accordingly their level of support for the government, the latter will favour relaxed budget spending. As a consequence, necessary austerity policies in order to strengthen the stability of a fixed exchange-rate regime in ERM II may be delayed too long [136]. A future devaluation becomes then even more likely.

For CEECs, the easiest way out of possible exchange-rate distress would be to jump into the euro at once. Hence, unilateral euroization is a regime, which is most effective in avoiding monetary turmoil.[13] This may be the overall objective with respect to a smooth transition of CEECs to the EMU, since a currency crisis heavily disrupts the integration process. Therefore, unilateral euroization is – at least, at first glance – the best choice for an exchange-rate regime with regard to

---

[12] Hallerberg and Vinhas de Souza [107] have searched for political business cycles in CEECs from 1990 to 1999. They empirically prove that the combination of capital mobility and fixed exchange rates renders an institutional arrangement, such as an independent central bank designed to deter governments from generating a political business cycle, redundant.

[13] This has been thought about currency boards, as well. However, the fall of Argentina's Peso in December 2001 indicates that currency board arrangements can also be doomed to fail. See, for example, Wójcik [213] for probably increasing countries' default risks in the course of unilateral euroization.

the elimination of exchange rate risks. Besides, there are some more microeconomic advantages, such as, the lowering of transaction costs and the transparency of prices. These would foster economic integration, both by increased trade and FDI as well as by improving access to foreign capital.[14] As with fixed exchange-rate regimes (see above), euroization as the tightest exchange-rate commitment may be advisable for extremely small open economies where trade is a considerable share of national income as is the case with the Baltic countries [152]. In such countries a relatively erratic exchange-rate performance would hamper stabilization efforts [28, 74]. Above all, the most striking difference to soft pegs with respect to policy-makers' incentive structures is that unilateral euroization can be very unpleasant for national voters. Potential detrimental social effects of international competition can hardly be dampened, thereby, provoking voter alienation. Yet the opposite applies to soft pegs. For this reason, policy makers with a sufficiently short time-horizon will most probably favour soft pegs instead of euroization.

Stipulating soft pegs in the context of ERM II and the quasi-insurance of a likely 'bail-out' may invite governments in CEECs to exhibit excessive moral hazard. Prior to their entrance to the EU, CEECs will probably excel at good conduct. After attaining access they may slacken the reins in terms of economic policy. According to Szapáry [197] such phenomenon is denoted as a 'weighing-in syndrome' [40].

Summarily, the prescribed soft pegs in ERM II provoke moral-hazard behaviour in several respects. Particularly from the political economy perspective, soft pegs allow for the usual political business cycle behaviour. Governments in CEECs make no exception in this respect. There exists a quasi natural affinity of those governments to ease fiscal and thus, exchange-rate policies. These political-economic considerations underpin the previously derived moral-hazard behaviour of CEECs with respect to the 'core' and the 'crux'.

---

[14] Certainly, there are also some costs of replacing the national currency by issuing the euro. The necessity of previously accumulating large scale currency reserves, the loss of instruments of cushioning exogenous shocks, the loss of seignorage, the loss of a lender of last resort etc are such examples. Whether a country should opt for unilateral euroization as net benefits are possibly positive is an empirical question [155]. Another serious problem that can arise in euroization – which also applies to fixing the conversion rates of CEECs' currencies vis a vis the euro – is misalignment. Any potential misalignment falls on the real economy. Because of nominal stickiness this can be at the expense of output and employment.

4.4 Results

To sum up, exchange-rate policies in CEEC are a 'hot potato' because soft pegs in ERM II are basically prone to speculative attacks particularly during the course of trend real appreciation. The progressive full liberalization of capital flows in a non-mature financial surrounding even exacerbates the likelihood of exchange rate crises. Thus, there is an impending risk of reversing capital inflows thereby, possibly deteriorating the overall European integration process. We have characterized this risk as the potential external effects of CEECs' exchange-rate policy formation.

Soft pegs exhibit some tempting incentives for policy-makers. From the perspective of political economy, politicians are most notably seeking to maximize votes. Soft pegs are really excellent in this regard as governments can comfort voters with more additional budget spending. This works as long as voters and politicians are not excessively inclined to a possible future breakdown of the exchange-rate regime. This moral-hazard problem is aggravated when CEECs are already credibly committed to joining the EMU. At the same time, current members of the EMU do not apparently dispose of effective countermeasures. Hence, CEECs can most probably not be prevented from making use of the risk of exchange-rate crises, but are likely to practise brinkmanship.

The implied costs of convergence during the Maastricht qualification process provide for a switch regarding the stance of exchange-rate policies in CEECs. The new members will probably make the most of the opportunity and threaten to put the entire enlargement process at risk by precipitating a currency crisis. In doing so, there is some leeway achieved in loading considerable costs of convergence onto current members of the EMU. In general, the ground for CEECs' moral-hazard behaviour is initially prepared by the 'core' and the 'crux' of the 'EU-enlargement' project (see Chap. 3). In addition, the trend real appreciation in CEECs, the stipulated crisis-prone soft pegs of ERM II, lacking institutional precautions in relevant European governance matters, and the impact of soft pegs on the incentive structure for policy-makers are conducive to CEECs' brinkmanship.

The exploration of exchange-rate policies in CEECs has shown that the prospective EMU-members have until now run exchange-rate regimes as an essential part of monetary policy aiming at disinflation. However, the discussion has also revealed that membership in ERM II can be a turning point in respective countries policy-choice. It has become evident that the national interests of prospective members can be in favour of a perilous track of exchange-rate policy making. In imitation of some features of a 'beggar-thy-neighbour' – i.e. passing costs on to other countries – exchange-rate policy in ERM II turns out to be a "threaten-thy-neighbour"-policy. The according brinkmanship is subject to the following game-theoretic analysis.

5

Game-Theoretic Analysis

This chapter explores the potential for conflict of transitory fixed exchange-rate arrangements in European integration process, in particular in the course of the adjustment process within ERM II. In doing so, we formalize the preceding considerations on moral-hazard behaviour and in particular the brinkmanship. This game-theoretic analysis determines the scope and limits of the brinkmanship. By the same token, the analysis inquires into alternative bargaining solutions for that conflict. It is shown to what extent CEECs can pass costs of convergence on to the EU-15. The entire game in the phase of ERM II consists of the brinkmanship and of the subsequent bargaining game. Accordingly, the final phase of investment into the 'EU-enlargement' project represents a two-stage threat game.

Moreover, we investigate different bargaining solutions concepts. Bargaining theory provides several bargaining solution concepts. In general, cooperative and non-cooperative bargaining games are distinguished from one another. In contrast to the contract curve in the Edgeworth box (see p. 23), which exhibits a good deal of possible solutions, bargaining-solution concepts offer unique solutions. Unfortunately, there are various solution concepts and, hence, many unique solutions. Each concept reflects applicable but different aspects of the bargaining situation. Each application depends on the presumed circumstances of negotiations. However, different bargaining solutions may yield different outcomes. Therefore, bargaining solutions are not necessarily interchangeable at will [108].

Nash [150] has been the first who put his solution concept up for discussion. The idea of this so-called Nash-programme is to ascertain general principles of solution concepts by studying different empirical phenomena. We take this idea into account as we use it to study the same bargaining situation from different angles of solution concepts. This heuristic course of action allows for reviewing the robustness of a predicted bargaining outcome: The more bargaining-solution concepts suggest an identical outcome at the same time, the more likely that outcome is.

The remainder of this chapter is structured as follows: First, basic characteristics of the two-stage threat game and the subsequent bargaining game are outlined. In doing so, assumptions are surveyed and the considerations of Sect. 3.1 are resumed. This allows for formalizing the brinkmanship. Second, alternative bargaining solution concepts are applied and studied in terms of the outlined Nash-programme. Finally, the discussion results in determining the most plausible equilibrium solution for the entire two-stage threat game.

5.1 Two-Stage Bargaining with Brinkmanship

The subsequent game G is part of the game H – i.e. the 'EU-enlargement' project resulting in the provision of the public good 'political stability' in the region CEE. The game H covers the period from Copenhagen 1993 up to the final introduction of the euro in the prospective EMU-member countries. The game G, however, only refers to the phase of CEECs as 'members with a derogation' which is basically the period of ERM II. The particular Maastricht qualification process, especially the phase of ERM II, is presented as two-stage threat game. Thus, it literally makes allowance for the 'threaten-thy-neighbour'-strategy, i.e. the brinkmanship. This brinkmanship game is characterized by complete but imperfect information. The investigation of strategic interaction – i.e. disputing the distribution of investment costs between $CEEC_i$ and EU-15 – occurs in two steps. First, the brinkmanship is elaborated in the form of a sequential game. Second, the subsequent bargaining for redistributing the costs of convergence is analysed. The latter is the subject matter of the next section.

Some premisses have to be put first: We base the two-stage threat game on the action of two players – i.e. a single $CEEC_i$ and the EU-15 with quasi-linear preferences for the public good 'political stability'.

The appropriateness of presuming quasi-linear actor preferences has been discussed in Sect. 3.1. We have applied such preferences to voters demanding particular policies. In the following game, CEECs' governments represent their voters' quasi-linear preferences.[1] According to

---

[1] The reader may note that we do not simply neglect the role of interest groups in the process of aggregating individual voter preferences. We conduct this

quasi-linearity voters provide a specific share of their income in exchange for the demanded provision of policies and public goods respectively. After having chosen a particular consumption level of public goods (policies) this specific demand is henceforth income invariant, i.e. there is no income effect. Accordingly, we can assume that the CEECs' further economic catching-up entirely flows into the demand for private goods. Hence, a single $CEEC_i$'s willingness to pay for completing the 'EU-enlargement' project and providing the public good 'political stability' does not change over time. Additionally, this property of quasi-linear preferences then allows for a later standardization of the brinkmanship game's pay-off structure.

The two-player assumption is, on the one hand, a concession to the subsequently deployed bargaining-solution concepts, i.e. a minimal common denominator. On the other hand, there are good arguments for proceeding with a two-player constellation instead of dealing with each of 25 EU-members individually.

In the subsequent bargaining game, we make use of the cooperative Nash-bargaining and the Kalai-Smorodinsky solution as well as the non-cooperative Ståhl-Rubinstein solution. All the bargaining solutions have been developed on basis of a two-player game. The problem, however, is that n-person extensions – in respect of the preceding order – are possible, impossible or implausible. Roth [173] has shown that a n-person extension of the Nash-bargaining solution is possible. However, this author also proves that the same does not apply to the Kalai-Smorodinsky solution [173]. At the same time, the literature provides some approaches to n-person extensions of the Ståhl-Rubinstein solution with unique equilibrium results [149]. These approaches rely, for instance, on a fixed order in alternating offers [15] or randomly selected proposers [16] and, in addition, on a stochastically altering size of the bargaining subject [139]. The latter assumption would be completely inappropriate for this two-stage threat game because the costs of convergence – i.e. bargaining subject (see below) – of leading CEECs towards EMU are discrete values and common knowledge. Presumptions in terms of fixed orders of alternating offers and randomly selected proposers have also to be rejected. The reason relates to the fact of competition among all CEECs: In respect of the delineated pay-off structure of the game $\Gamma(\varsigma_i, d)$ (see below), there is a chance for every single $CEEC_i$ that refrains from brinkmanship to come away empty-

---

rather simple kind of 'low-fat modelling' because of the specific characteristics of exchange-rate policies – i.e. concerning large sections of the electorate instead of particular special interests.

handed. This is to say, that this country misses any compensation when EU-15 is in a position to provide financial assistance in particular cases, i.e. solely for CEECs that practise brinkmanship. For that reason, we conceptualize a single $CEEC_i$ that rather hurries to brinkmanship. At the same time, it seems to be quite legitimate to consider a unitary player EU-15. This is because all current members of EMU have the common interest of rather disliking to share a $CEEC_i$'s costs of convergence. For that reason, we design the passing through as a two-player game.

A finite sequential threat game $G = (S_{(i)j}, u_{(i)j})^2_{j=1}$ is played. The two risk-neutral[2] players are a $CEEC_i$ (denoted as player $j = 1$, whereas $i = 1, ..., n$) and the EU-15 (player $j = 2$) with quasi-linear preferences for the public good 'political stability'. In addition, we assign both players the same level of bargaining power, where α_i is the bargaining power of a $CEEC_i$ and β_{-i} the particular corresponding bargaining power of an EU-15 with $\alpha_i = \beta_{-i}$, $\alpha_i + \beta_{-i} = 1$.[3] All parameters are common knowledge, which is a basic assumption for the application of the Rubinstein concept. The players' strategy sets in G are denoted $S_i = S_{i1} \times S_2$ with the pay-offs $u_{(i)j} : S_i \to \mathbb{R}^2$.

Both players haggle over sharing the costs of convergence. These costs are the Maastricht costs of convergence denoted as C_i^C for a specific $CEEC_i$. The C_i^C are leftovers for bargaining in the phase of ERM II. There have been considerable costs for $CEEC_i$ and EU-15 up to then. In Sect. 3.1 we have set forth that these are sunk costs. The same discussion has also shown that bearing the entire C_i^C reflects each player's maximum willingness to pay for a successful passing through the phase of ERM II. The according benefits with respect to a single $CEEC_i$ are denoted here as B_i.[4] These benefits stand for completing the 'EU enlargement' project and ensuring the provision of the public good 'political stability' in CEE. In line with this reasoning, ev-

---

[2] In general, risk-preferences affect each player's perceived value – i.e. pay-off – of a possible outcome. The following game-theoretic discussion is simplified in terms of presuming risk-neutral players. However, given the size of the actors involved the assumption of risk neutrality is standard.

[3] The term 'bargaining power' is best understood as talent for negotiating or a player's skill in duping the other [151]. Although it seems to be the fact that 'bargaining power' is mixed with power indices (meaning a player's influence on decision-making outcomes) we stick to this more traditional reading of 'talent for negotiating'.

[4] The reader may note that we make concessions to our conceptualization of a two-player game in form of explicitly modelling the benefits of the public good 'political stability' as a two-player affair. For that reason, we add a subscript i to the according benefits.

ery candidate country is equally indifferent regarding admittance and non-admittance to EMU in instances of bearing C_i^C entirely alone as stipulated by the Treaty establishing the European Community. This also applies to the EU-15: The EU-15 will never pay more than total C_i^C to a single CEEC$_i$. Bearing the entire burden of the CEEC$_i$'s costs of convergence makes the EU-15 just as indifferent to the accession and non-accession of CEEC$_i$. This trick of standardization allows for a specific adaption of the two-stage threat game G that considerably simplifies further analysis. By the same token, the modified game becomes empirically tractable.

Bargaining for costs of convergence resembles a simple 'splitting-of-the-pie'- or here more appropriately a 'dividing-the-euro'-game. The basic difference is that both players do not maximize their piece of the pie, but minimize their respective share of costs of convergence. The present bargaining problem is characterized by the tuple $(\mathbb{C}_i, d)$ where $\mathbb{C}_i \subset \mathbb{R}^2$ is a vector combination of feasible (dis-)utility allocations. The disagreement point d is the bargaining outcome if both parties do not come to an agreement and negotiations break down. In that case, markets will notice that CEEC$_i$ and EU-15 cannot agree on an appropriate policy mix for CEEC$_i$ in ERM II. This will trigger a speculative attack, and an exchange-rate crisis ensues entailing costs of default C_i^D – i.e. output loss in an exchange-rate crisis' aftermath.

Figure 5.1 drafts one version of the subsequent bargaining.[5]

The following costs arise in this game: First, there are the above-mentioned 'costs of convergence' C_i^C – i.e. the entailing output gap during the rigourous compliance with the Maastricht criteria. According to the rationale of the Maastricht qualification process, it seems natural that CEEC$_i$ bears such costs entirely alone – denoted by stage 1 in Fig. 5.1. The C_i^C are what the bargaining revolves around. If CEEC$_i$ succeeds in the bargaining – i.e. to pass some costs of convergence on to EU-15 – the game results in the new equilibrium of stage 2 (see 5.1). If the according negotiations on distributing C_i^C were to break down, then an exchange-rate crisis will occur and both players will be stuck with the disagreement point d. The standard assumption holds that $\mathbb{C}_i$ is a non-empty, convex and compact set.

The question arises to what extent the EU-15 pays for CEECs. A currency crisis entails above all costs for CEEC$_i$. However, the EU-15 can

---

[5] This figure just depicts one possible solution. There are alternative bargaining solutions that also rely upon a specific subsidiary role of the EU-15 (see below).

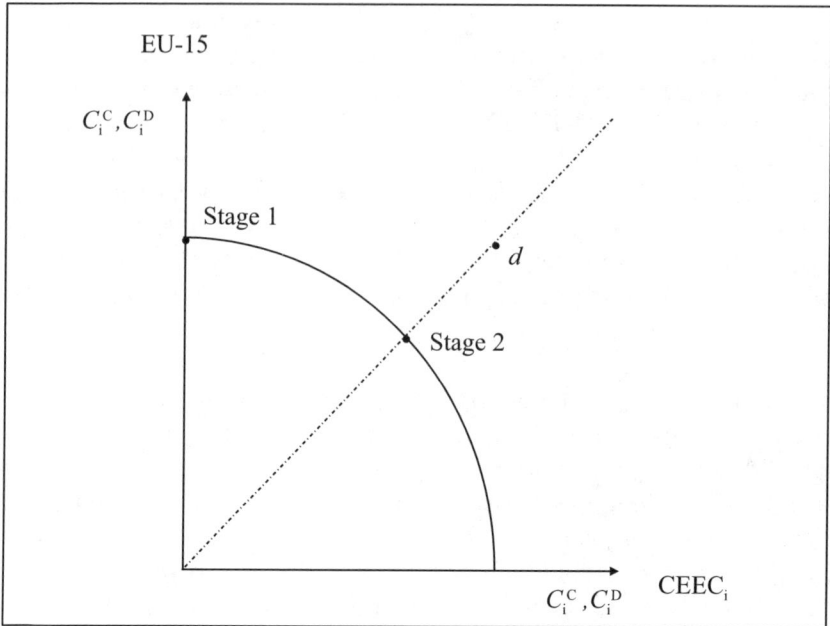

Fig. 5.1. Bargaining for costs of convergence

also suffer from rising costs. When a $CEEC_i$ experiences excessive output losses, they are automatically considered for additional funds in terms of European Regional and Structural Policy and the Common Agricultural Policy. Even more important in this context is the CEECs' potential for drawing out and blocking decision-making processes in all European policy fields. This generally applies as soon as the CEECs become EU-members. Given a serious negative impact of exchange-rate crises on political stability due to infuriated voters resisting further European integration, the EU-15 will provide extra-funding. However, the EU-15 has a particular subsidiary role: When a currency crisis occurs, then $CEEC_i$ will first and foremost have to bear the burden of the costs. Albeit, $CEEC_i$ will not accept costs higher than total C_i^C. Hence, if $C_i^D > C_i^C$, then the EU-15 will have to administer financial assistance within the limits of their maximum willingness to pay. Accordingly, the EU-15 will have limited liability amounting to the share λ_i of total C_i^C with $0 \leq \lambda_i \leq 1$. This is to say, that the EU-15 will at most transfer funds amounting to a total of C_i^C to $CEEC_i$. If it were that $C_i^D \leq C_i^C$, then $CEEC_i$ would have no potential threat at its disposal. A $CEEC_i$ would come away empty handed. Such a $CEEC_i$ would not be eligible for the brinkmanship. The following proposition can be derived from these considerations:

$$\lambda_i = \begin{cases} 0 & \text{if } C_i^C \geq C_i^D \\ 0 < \lambda_i < 1 & \text{if } C_i^C < C_i^D < 2C_i^C \\ 1 & \text{else} \end{cases} . \tag{5.1}$$

The idea of the brinkmanship is that $CEEC_i$ threatens to realize the overall worst pay-off represented in the disagreement point d. In doing so, it can under identifiable conditions redistribute some costs of convergence (C_i^C). Apart from the structure of costs the marginal conditions of the threat game are of interest. First, $CEEC_i$ must have the capacity to control a gradual escalation of risk to some extent. Although, some uncertainty and forms of irreversibility have to remain. As with 'Schelling', $CEEC_i$ creates an advantageous bargaining position for itself by making sure that it will not retreat. In this context, irreversibility means making statements about its relative evaluation of disagreement and agreement – i.e. that it cannot comfortably retract from a commitment.[6] Additionally, markets need to respond to changes in economic policy formation in $CEEC_i$. If markets remain absolutely non-reactive, then there will be no scope for any political manoeuvrers by $CEEC_i$. In that case, a prospective EMU-member must choose between rigourous compliance with Maastricht criteria and practising an optimal national policy mix. In instances of the latter, they would certainly avoid any costs of convergence, but they would not be admitted to the EMU, thereby not realizing the mutually beneficial investment project 'EU enlargement'.

Successful brinkmanship is especially dependent on the two given probabilities p and q_i that are independent of each other and endogenous – i.e. it is the cost structure that determines their values. From the perspective of $CEEC_i$, p denotes the probability of encountering a frugal EU-15. The more frugal the EU-15, the lower the likelihood for a successful brinkmanship. At this point, we take into account that $CEEC_i$ will already be an EU-member and has a say in European decision-making. In order to ensure smooth functioning within the EU, an EU-15 may view the making of side payments as an indispensable tool when

---

[6] For example, an announced shift in monetary and fiscal policy affairs should be in fact reversible. But repealing an announced or even previously introduced law – for instance, a Christmas bonus for unemployed farmers – will be most probably uncomfortable for parties in parliament. This fact corresponds to the aforementioned 'audience costs' which are generated in order to bolster a threat (see p. 33.)

seeking a $CEEC_i$'s consent to an agreement. For that reason, values of
$p < 1$. At the same time $p > 0$, because no rational actor is keen on
just spending his money abroad without acquiring satisfying returns.
Accordingly, corner solutions of p can be clearly rejected and, hence,
$0 < p < 1$. The probability q_i basically describes the likelihood of provoking an exchange-rate crisis in terms of withdrawing public approval
in the present exchange-rate policy stance. In this respect, q_i makes
allowances for alternative elasticities of voters' reactions in $CEEC_i$ to
altering costs of convergence C_i^C. We presume that national voters in
new member countries react to arising costs of convergence. Voters con-
stantly weigh the costs against the potential benefits of EMU-accession.
If they were apathetic, then policy-makers – aggregating voters' preferences – would simply never have to decide between the advantages
of maintaining a central parity and the possible disadvantages in terms
of reducing the likelihood of their re-election. This is not a realistic
scenario. Consequently, we make allowance for governments weighing
the advantages of maintaining an existing exchange-rate regime against
the hardship of voter alienation. This is the 'Obstfeld' trade-off that
markets test for when practising a speculative attack (see Sect. 2.3).
When such trade-off is absent neither a reversal of capital flows, nor
speculative attacks may be triggered: the probability q_i for devaluation
would be zero. However, voters' respective governments must also rank
the benefits B_i as valuable. Otherwise, they would never accept any
costs of convergence. In this case, the according risk of devaluation,
and subsequent exchange-rate crisis would be 1. In all instances, we
presume that voters, like governments and markets, perceive trade-offs.
Correspondingly, we exclude corner solutions for q_i, thus $0 < q_i < 1$.

Basing exchange-rate policy on a quasi-adventuresome strategy of
brinkmanship is like walking a dangerous tightrope. However, if these
conditions for successful brinkmanship are met – i.e. the threat is a
deterrent strategy, – then the EU-15 will dance obligingly to $CEEC_i$'s
tune. The bargaining will result in the new equilibrium of stage 2, where
$CEEC_i$'s share of total C_i^C is minimized (cf. Fig. 5.1 on p. 80). The EU-
15 bears the burden a corresponding share c_i of costs of convergence
C_i^C. In this situation $CEEC_i$ is indifferent towards the employment
of brinkmanship and keeping track of the prescribed passing through
the phase of ERM II. In the following, we explore the mutually best
responses (i.e. Nash-strategies) which will in the end constitute a sub-
game perfect Nash equilibrium of the two-stage threat game.

Figure 5.2 presents the extensive form of the threat game G. It illustrates the possible game outcomes and shows how the 'threaten-thy-neighbour'-strategy works.

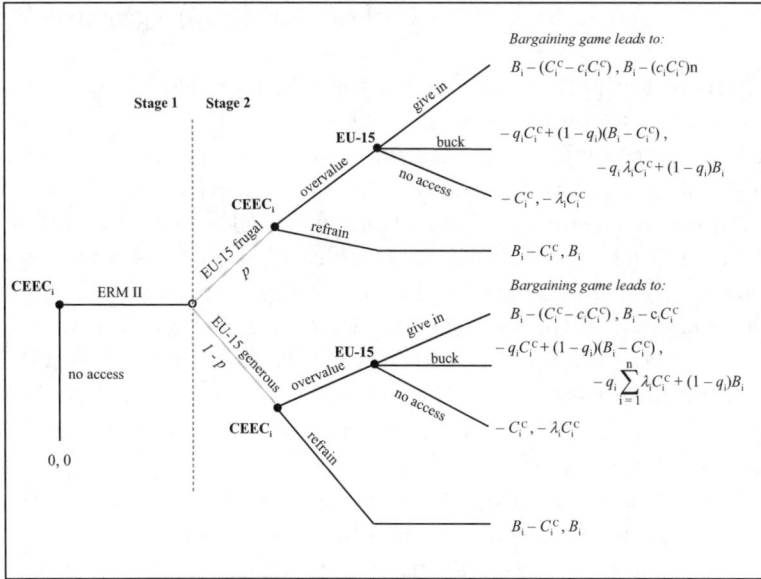

Bargaining game leads to:

$$B_i - (C_i^c - c_i C_i^c), B_i - (c_i C_i^c)n$$

$$-q_i C_i^c + (1 - q_i)(B_i - C_i^c),$$

$$-q_i \lambda_i C_i^c + (1 - q_i)B_i$$

$$-C_i^c, -\lambda_i C_i^c$$

$$B_i - C_i^c, B_i$$

Bargaining game leads to:

$$B_i - (C_i^c - c_i C_i^c), B_i - c_i C_i^c$$

$$-q_i C_i^c + (1 - q_i)(B_i - C_i^c),$$

$$-q_i \sum_{i=1}^{n} \lambda_i C_i^c + (1 - q_i)B_i$$

$$-C_i^c, -\lambda_i C_i^c$$

$$B_i - C_i^c, B_i$$

Fig. 5.2. Two-stage bargaining with brinkmanship

Apart from the above-mentioned costs, two different sub-games due to imperfect information have to be taken into consideration. Prior to choosing a strategy, $CEEC_i$ does not know whether it will encounter a frugal or a generous EU-15. In this context, specific costs of default have to be distinguished. On the one hand, a single crisis has the potential to spread like wildfire through all n $CEEC_i$. From the perspective of the EU-15 this would be the overall worst pay-off (see second branch of the lower sub game in Fig. 5.2). Fearing such exorbitant costs the primary goal would be to maintain public support in each $CEEC_i$ by any means necessary. From this point of view, it may be more beneficial to be generous rather than to spoil the entire process of European integration. On the other hand, the EU-15 may also display a rather reluctant attitude towards providing extra-funding. In this case the EU-15 may be mindful of the proverb, 'If you give an inch they will take a mile'. This is to say, that the provision of extra-funding for a single $CEEC_i$ will possibly entail further payments to other $CEEC_i$, for instance, due to the principle belief that all EU-members should be treated equally.[7] Accordingly, the EU-15 would have to transfer n-times of C_i^C (see upper branch of the upper sub game in Fig. 5.2). Due to the present uncertainty concerning the EU-15's attitude towards providing extra-funding, the pay-offs for $CEEC_i$ have to be weighted with a probability p for encountering a frugal respectively $(1-p)$ a generous EU-15.

In regard to the players' strategies, the $CEEC_i$'s feasible set of strategies in stage 1 is comprised of two choices: 'the ERM II' – i.e. to enter the convergence play – thus entering stage 2, or can choose 'no access'. In this case, it would forgo the benefits of integration B_i – i.e. adopting the euro thus ensuring the completion of the 'EU-enlargement' project. However, if such a decision is made $CEEC_i$ would have zero cost of convergence, because it resorted to an optimal national policy mix. If $CEEC_i$ chooses 'no access' the EU-15 would neither receive B_i, nor be confronted with possibly providing extra-funding for $CEEC_i$. This applies, because we rule out the possibility of default when $CEEC_i$ is following an optimal national policy mix. A respective economic policy formation would definitely exclude the alienation of voters and consequently speculative attacks. After having chosen 'ERM II', $CEEC_i$ implements a policy mix that satisfies the Maastricht obligations.[8] This policy mix cannot be altered during stage 2 – i.e. costs of convergence C_i^C will arise in any case. In stage 2, $CEEC_i$ can choose to 'refrain' and 'overvalue', i.e. to pursue a brinkmanship strategy by aggravating the trend real appreciation and the according devaluation risk. However, in doing so the brinkmanship is limited to *threatening* to 'overvalue'. Brinkmanship is based on this kind of uncertainty.[9] Respective fiscal measures are announced, but not yet implemented. If implemented, this would indeed trigger a speculative attack and a subsequent devaluation. In this case, the $CEEC_i$'s strategy of brinkmanship would have failed.

---

[7] For example, the brinkmanship may result in a new institutional scheme of 'economic and social cohesion', which would be represented here in the specific monetary terms. Note that $CEEC_i$ will already be an EU-member at that stage.

[8] In stage 1, we simply act as if the current members of the EMU have no say in deciding whether $CEEC_i$ enters ERM II or not. This is on no account arbitrary: Even if the current members of the EMU would deny $CEEC_i$ access to the ERM II, sovereign 'members with a derogation' could certainly resort to crises-prone fixed exchange-rate regimes.

[9] Wagner [204] and Powell [166] portray the Cuban missile crisis as an instance of real-life brinkmanship. They develop a vivid example of dealings with uncertainty in a brinkmanship game.

Due to the multiple-equilibria presumption, a current exchange-rate policy formation – i.e. the underlying fiscal and monetary policy mix – may be deemed unsustainable with the exchange-rate regime in place. An originally sound economic policy formation may at a moment's notice roll over and trigger a speculative attack (see Sect. 2.3). Hence, in view of possibly disastrous fiscal policy the players' reactions will likely be immediate. If $CEEC_i$ choose to not 'overvalue' – i.e. not to slacken the reins in fiscal affairs, or practise benign neglect concerning its fundamentals, – those considerations will still hold true when $CEEC_i$ undergoes an exogenous shock. Then, the prospective member country would still need to weigh the advantages and disadvantages of preserving an existing exchange-rate regime.

If $CEEC_i$ refrains from the brinkmanship, it forgoes the opportunity to load costs of convergence C_i^C onto the EU-15. This would be the best pay-off from the perspective of the EU-15 as stage 1 of the brinkmanship game would remain unchanged. When $CEEC_i$ resorts to the brinkmanship – i.e. choosing 'overvalue', – the outcome ultimately depends on the reaction of the EU-15 can choose a strategy of 'give in' when $CEEC_i$ overvalues or it can 'buck', i.e. to withhold any payments. Furthermore, it can also choose a strategy of 'no access' – i.e. to cut $CEEC_i$'out.

Before elaborating on the pay-off structure of game G, we can make a simplification: Given that both players' maximum willingness to pay for integration – i.e. realizing the benefits B_i of introducing the euro and in this way the completion of the 'EU-enlargement' project – corresponds to the total C_i^C, we can normalize $C_i^C = B_i = 1$. In accordance with the rationale of section 3.1, we now transform the brinkmanship game G: In accordance with the preceding discussion, the subsequent bargaining game has the form of $\Gamma(\varsigma_i, d)$ with $0 \leq c_{ij} \leq 1$, $c_{ij} \in \varsigma_i$, $\varsigma_i \subset \mathbb{R}^2$. A specific property of Γ is that its strategy set $\varsigma_i \subset S_i$. The according equilibrium solution of this particular game Γ is of special interest for our analysis.

The pay-offs for specific strategy combinations in stage 2 – the values for the pay-offs in stage 1 remain unchanged – are as portrayed in Fig. 5.3.

In this game $\Gamma(\varsigma_i, d)$ $CEEC_i$ maximizes the EU-15's share c_i. The bargaining leads to a new outcome c_i for $CEEC_i$ in stage 2. At the same time, $CEEC_i$ burdens the EU-15, in turn, with the remaining share $1 - c_i$. Accordingly, the players' continuous utility functions $u_{(i)j}(c_{(i)j})$ are:

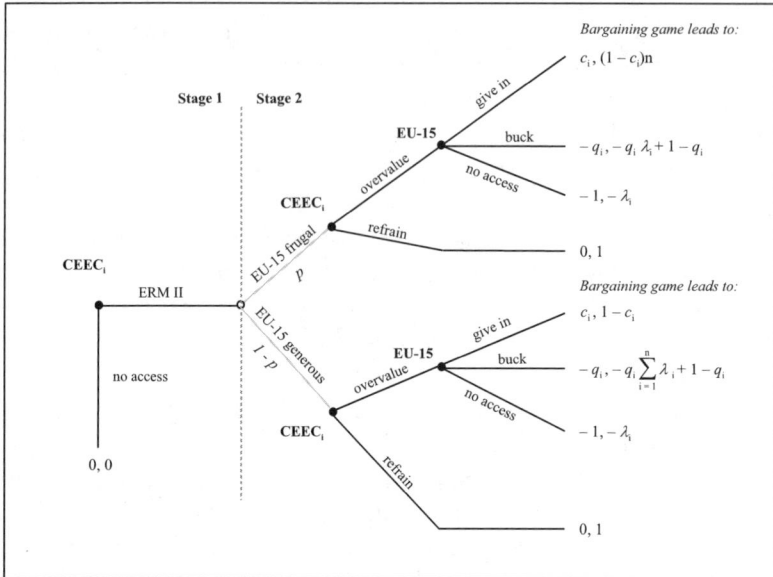

Fig. 5.3. Transformed two-stage bargaining with brinkmanship

$$u_{i1}(c_{i1}) = c_{i1} = c_i \tag{5.2}$$

$$u_2(c_{i2}) = c_{i2} = (1 - c_i) . \tag{5.3}$$

The disagreement point d represents the $CEEC_i$'s threat, where the pay-off is $(-1, -\lambda_i)$ similar in Fig. 5.3 to the case of 'no access'. As with G, the game $\Gamma(\varsigma_i, d)$ in stage 2 ends with bargaining on the non-empty, convex and compact set comprising any convex combination of $c_{ij} = (c_{i1}, c_{i2})$.

The pay-offs are as follows: If $CEEC_i$ chooses a strategy of 're-frain' – i.e. does not practise brinkmanship, – then it receives zero, whereat the EU-15 gets 1. If $CEEC_i$ chooses to 'overvalue', the EU-15 can 'give in', 'buck' or choose 'no access'. When EU-15 gives in, then $CEEC_i$ receives the aspired alleviation in amount of c_i. From the perspective of the EU-15 the pay-off is $(1 - c_i)$, and consists of the remaining costs of convergence which are not accepted by $CEEC_i$. Although, the EU-15 may also have to deal with transferring payments to all $CEEC_i$ amounting to n times the size of $(1 - c_i)$. If the EU-15 chooses to 'buck', $CEEC_i$ may be stuck with costs of default amounting to $(-q_i)$. Simultaneously, the EU-15 receives the pay-off $(-q_i\lambda_i + 1 - q_i)$ respectively $(-q_i \sum_{i=1}^{n} \lambda_i + 1 - q_i)$ in the case of contagion among all

$CEEC_i$. If the EU-15 chooses 'no access' after $CEEC_i$ has introduced the 'threaten-thy-neighbour'-strategy, then both players will realize the worst outcome, at which both will be left without the completion of the 'EU-enlargement' project. At the same time $CEEC_i$ will have to bear the burden of the full costs of convergence (because altering a once implemented policy mix is impossible), receiving (-1), whereas the EU-15 receives a pay-off of $(-\lambda_i)$. This pay-off is the same as in the breaking off of negotiations, i.e. the disagreement point d.

A 'threaten-thy-neighbour'-strategy has to satisfy some necessary conditions. In particular, a successful brinkmanship has to meet a condition of effectiveness and acceptability. The effectiveness of such brinkmanship rests on the extent of $CEEC_i$'s default: as the EU-15 is increasingly affected by costs, a $CEEC_i$'s threat gains more credibility. That is to say, that the probability of a currency crisis arising is subject to a critical threshold. If the respective probability is too small, the EU-15 cannot be coerced into providing assistance. However, the credibility of the brinkmanship strategy is also dependent on whether the outcome is acceptable to $CEEC_i$. If the probability of an exchange-rate crisis is too high, then $CEEC_i$ will abstain from a hazardous exchange-rate policy.

The $CEEC_i$'s brinkmanship will be successful – i.e. eliciting the desired extra funds amounting to c_i, – if it constitutes a deterrent threat. In this regard, successful brinkmanship is dependent on the conditions of effectiveness and acceptability. $CEEC_i$'s brinkmanship may be effective, if – from the perspective of the EU-15 – the expected pay-off from a choice to 'give in' was higher than a decision to 'buck' when taking into account possible contagion. Therefore,

$$(-q_i \sum_{i=1}^{n} \lambda_i + 1 - q_i) < (1 - c_i) .$$

Accordingly, the minimum probability $q_{i,min}$ has to be

$$q_{i,min} > \frac{c_i}{\sum_{i=1}^{n} \lambda_i + 1} . \qquad (5.4)$$

The probability $q_{i,min}$ for currency crisis in $CEEC_i$ is the lower bound of the brinkmanship. Below this level the EU-15 would choose a strategy of 'buck', even if it is generous.

However, when encountering a more frugal EU-15 – which will be encountered with a probability of p – $CEEC_i$ may feel that a strategy of 'overvalue' is too risky. Accordingly, the acceptability condition would not be met: $CEEC_i$ will encounter a generous EU-15 with a probability of $(1 - p)$, which will choose a strategy of 'give in' when the effectiveness condition holds. Thus, for a given $0 < q_i < 1$ $CEEC_i$ will pose a probabilistic threat, if its expected pay-off is higher than a zero pay-off from a strategy of 'refraining':

$$(-q_i p) + c_i(1 - p) > 0 .$$

After resolving we obtain

$$q_{i,max} < c_i \frac{1 - p}{p} . \tag{5.5}$$

Accordingly, the acceptability condition depends on values for p and the prospective bargaining solution c_i. This indicates that there must be a bargaining pay-off $c_i \neq 0$. Otherwise, any brinkmanship would be fruitless from the beginning because the acceptability condition would require that $q_{i,max} < 0$, which is impossible and contradicts the exclusion of corner solutions.

The values for p have to be below a critical threshold. Otherwise, $q_{i,max}$ would have to be smaller than $q_{i,min}$ for some high values of p. That would render any brinkmanship fruitless – i.e. effective, but not acceptable because the likelihood of encountering a frugal EU-15 would be too high. From the proposition $q_{i,min} < q_{i,max}$ it follows that the upper bound is

$$p_{max} < \frac{\sum_{i=1}^{n} \lambda_i + 1}{\sum_{i=1}^{n} \lambda_i + 2} < 1 . \tag{5.6}$$

However, there is also a type of lower bound. If the probability p for encountering a frugal EU-15 is very small, $CEEC_i$ will always find the brinkmanship acceptable. This holds when

$$c_i \frac{1 - p}{p} \geq 1 .$$

Hence, 'threaten-thy-neighbour' is always acceptable for critical values

$$p_i^0 \leq \frac{c_i}{c_i + 1} . \tag{5.7}$$

If the probability p for a frugal EU-15 satisfies the acceptability condition, then the following proposition must be valid:

$$p^* \in P^*, \qquad P^* := \{p^* \,|\, p^* < p_{max} < 1, \, p^* \in \mathbb{R}_+^*\} . \tag{5.8}$$

In the end, the probability q_i in the brinkmanship strategy has to remain below the critical threshold $q_{i,max}$, above that value CEEC$_i$ will refrain from a strategy of 'overvalue', because it fears mutual detrimental effects. Therefore, for every given probability $\bar{p}^*$ the probabilistic threat is credible when a country-specific q_i^* is an element of the finite set Q_i^*. The according proposition is:

$$q_i^* \in Q_i^*, \qquad Q_i^* := \{q_i^* \mid q_{i,min} < q_i^* < q_{i,max}, \, q_i^* \in \mathbb{R}_+^*\} \, . \tag{5.9}$$

Both the parameters p and q_i determine whether a CEEC$_i$ is to practise brinkmanship. When the effectiveness and acceptability conditions – i.e. propositions (5.4) and (5.5) – are satisfied, the CEEC$_i$ will indeed practise a strategy of 'overvalue', i.e. our 'threaten-thy-neighbour'-policy. The CEEC$_i$ disposes of a deterrent threat, which provides leverage in the bargaining process for redistributing the costs of convergence shifting the outcome from stage 1 to stage 2 as in Fig. 5.1 (see p. 80). The EU-15's response to CEEC$_i$'s brinkmanship is to immediately burden itself with costs of convergence amounting to the share c_i. Thus, CEEC$_i$ passes the respective costs of convergence onto current members of the EMU. When receiving c_i, CEEC$_i$ will abstain from further attempts to promote a hazardous exchange-rate policy in ERM II and will behave well. CEEC$_i$ will then push through Maastricht criteria, since there are no further opportunities to pass costs onto current members of the EMU. This is because at that point their willingness to pay for the realization of the joint investment project 'EU enlargement' – i.e. providing the public good political stability in CEE – is exhausted. Both players will choose Nash-strategies reciprocally. Thus, there is a unique sub-game perfect Nash equilibrium in this brinkmanship game for the strategy combination of (('ERM II', 'overvalue'), 'give in').

There is also a graphical solution for this two-stage threat game (see Fig. 5.4).

The horizontal axis is the probability p of encountering a frugal EU-15, and the vertical axis is the probability q_i of provoking a currency crisis deteriorating the 'EU-enlargement' project and the public good 'political stability' respectively. In Fig. 5.4 the hyperbola describes the acceptability condition ($q_{i,max}$), whereas the horizontal line at $q_i = q_{i,min}$ depicts the effectiveness condition. The area left from the vertical line through p^0 covers all brinkmanship strategies that are always acceptable for CEEC$_i$. All in all, the area that is enclosed by the vertical axis, the horizontal line of $q_{i,min}$, the hyperbola, and the imagined ceiling at $q_i = 1$ contains all equilibrium solutions for successful

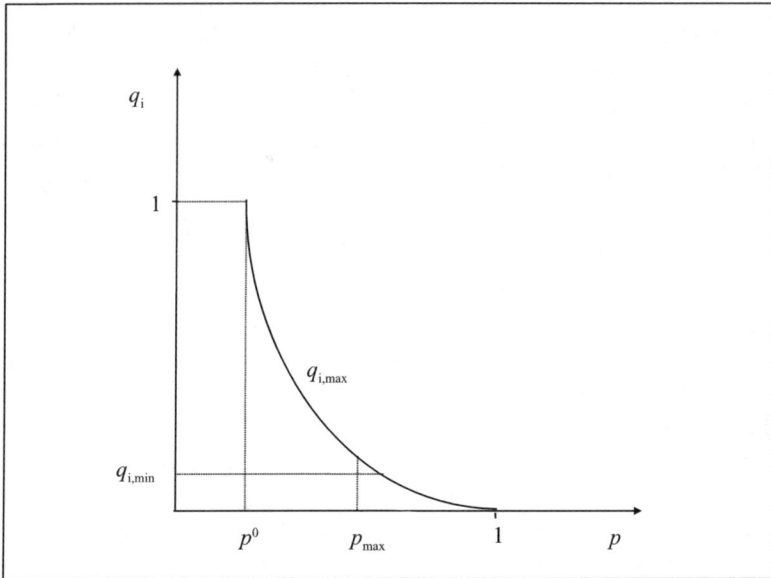

Fig. 5.4. Outline for a graphical solution of brinkmanship

brinkmanship. This is all combinations of the probabilities $\bar{p}^*$ q_i^* for a deterrent threat of the strategy combination (('ERM II', 'overvalue'), 'give in').

In the following paragraphs, we weaken possible reservations about the suggested design of the brinkmanship game. Following these explanations we survey alternative bargaining solutions.

Reservations regarding the delineated basic characteristics of this brinkmanship game are as follows: First, the question that mainly arises is whether the CEECs should form a (costly) cartel in order to intensify the threatening gesture. Second, one may state that the EU-15 can announce in advance that they will heavily punish the first country which dares to practise brinkmanship. This is to say, that current members of the EMU pursue an enter-deterrence game. Regarding the latter we simply presume that such course of EU-15's policy action conflicts with the principle of equal treatment. Therefore, the occurrence of an enter-deterrence game is rather implausible.

With regard to the CEECs' incentives to form a cartel we simply conjecture that each single CEEC$_i$ will be most anxious to signal that it does everything in its power to comply with Maastricht criteria. In turn,

CEEC$_i$ runs short of financing any costs of forming and maintaining a cartel. The vulnerable point of cartelization is the impact of international coordination on policy and market reactions. If it is becomes evident that some CEECs – i.e. countries that are 'unwilling' but not 'unable' to Maastricht criteria – explicitly coordinate their 'mis-policy efforts' than this will allow the EU-15 as well as markets to discriminate between these mis-behaving and other well-behaving CEECs. Accordingly, only the former will experience a speculative attack. A group of such 'depraved' CEECs is poorly advised to develop initiatives that allow the EU-15 and markets to discriminate. Such strategy is not in the slightest a sophisticated policy stance of manoeuvring on the brink of disaster, but a direct plunge into an abyss. It is necessary to build up a deterrent threat instead of an inevitable default.

Summarily, the phase of ERM II – as well as transitory exchange-rate arrangements in the course of EU-enlargement processes in general – has the potential for serious political conflict. The two-stage threat game appropriately depicts the constellation of CEECs as 'members with a derogation' coming up to full EMU-membership. Instead of simply adhering to the Maastricht provisions, CEECs are better off by utilizing the perverted incentive structure within the framework of ERM II. In the following section, we focus on the actual bargaining situation.

5.2 Alternative Bargaining Solutions

This section deals with the second part of the two-stage bargaining with the brinkmanship. At this stage of the game-theoretic analysis we inquire into alternative bargaining solutions. In particular, the Nash-Bargaining solution (NBS), the Kalai-Smorodinsky solution (KSS), and the Ståhl-Rubinstein solution (SRS) are studied. The different solutions concepts are studied in the above-mentioned order. In each instance, the relevance and the appropriateness of a solution concept to our bargaining situation are considered.[10] The goal of this course of action is to reach a robust bargaining outcome. In addition, we simultaneously determine both players' actual – instead of their maximum – willingness to pay for the public good 'political stability' (see Sect. 3.1).

---

[10] Note that we do not discuss the axioms of these bargaining solution concepts in the strict sense of the Nash-programme. Besides, the NBS is discussed more extensively. This allows, in turn, to reduce the subsequent representations of the KSS and the SRS.

5.2.1 Nash-Bargaining Solution

In general, the NBS [151, 150] has been the first bargaining solution ever. The bargaining is characterized by complete information. It is finite in that only one offer – and no counter-offers – are possible when bargaining. The bargaining revolves around arguing over sharing the expenses of the initial investment costs of the 'EU enlargement' project. Given that all specifics of the game are common knowledge, the players look ahead and anticipate reciprocal best responses. Due to this property of backward induction, negotiation time is irrelevant. The bargaining game comes to an immediate solution. It is also worth noting in this context that perfect commitment in the sense of cooperative bargaining theory is assumed. This is to say, that once bargaining outcomes are agreed upon the decision is binding. In regard to the pay-off structures, we still assume risk-neutral players. The concept of the NBS also presumes that these risk preferences are public knowledge. Accordingly, the Pareto-efficient solutions of the bargaining – i.e. moving on the convex hull in Fig. 5.5 – constitute a unique Nash equilibrium [55].

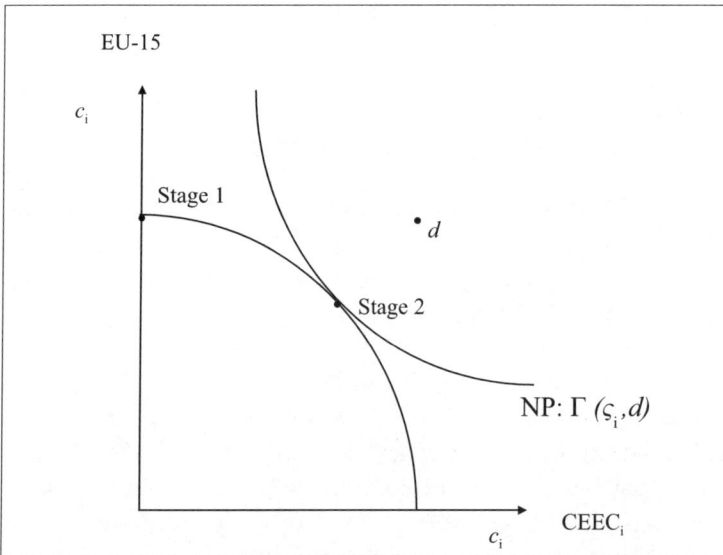

Fig. 5.5. Nash-Bargaining solution

The players' utility from splitting the costs of convergence corresponds to the other player's share of the costs. That is $CEEC_i$ maximizes the EU-15's share c_{i2}, which then leaves c_{i1} to the $CEEC_i$ and vice versa. The NBS is derived from the weighted Nash-product (NP) (see the hyperbola in Fig. 5.5):

$$\max_{c_{ij}} NP(\Gamma(\varsigma_i, d)) = (u_{i1}(c_{i1}) - u_{i1}(d_1))^{\alpha_i}(u_2(c_{i2}) - u_2(d_2))^{\beta_{-i}} \quad (5.10)$$

with $c_{ij} \geq d_j$, $c_{ij} \in \varsigma_i$, where α_i is the bargaining power of a $CEEC_i$ and β_{-i} the particular corresponding bargaining power of an EU-15 (see p. 78).[11]

Given the players' utility functions ((5.2) and (5.3) on p. 86) the maximization problem in light of $d = (-1, -\lambda_i)$ is:

$$\max_{c_{i1}, c_{i2}} \Gamma(\varsigma_i, d) = (c_i + 1)^{\alpha_i}((1 - c_i) + \lambda_i)^{\beta_{-i}} . \quad (5.11)$$

By substituting and taking into account that c_i^* has to be on the convex hull – i.e. using a Lagrangian multiplier – the according first-order condition is at last

$$\frac{dNP}{dc_i} = \alpha_i(c_i + 1)^{\alpha_i - 1}((1 - c_i) + \lambda_i))^{\beta_{-i}} -$$

$$- (c_i + 1)^{\alpha_i}\beta_{-i}((1 - c_i) + \lambda_i)^{\beta_{-i} - 1} = 0 .$$

After rearranging and accounting for a generalized equilibrium solution – i.e. taking into account different combinations of the bargaining powers α_i and β_{-i} – we receive the NBS

$$c_i^* = \begin{cases} 0 & \text{if } \dfrac{(1 + \lambda_i)\alpha_i - \beta_{-i}}{\alpha_i + \beta_{-i}} \leq 0 \\[2ex] 0 < c_i \leq 1 \text{ if } 0 < \dfrac{(1 + \lambda_i)\alpha_i - \beta_{-i}}{\alpha_i + \beta_{-i}} \leq 1 \\[2ex] 1 & \text{else } \dfrac{(1 + \lambda_i)\alpha_i - \beta_{-i}}{\alpha_i + \beta_{-i}} > 1 \end{cases} \quad (5.12)$$

Here, it becomes obvious that the EU-15's actual willingness to pay for $CEEC_i$'s integration depends on the distribution of bargaining power: Not surprisingly, the less bargaining power β_{-i} the EU-15 exhibit, the higher the values for c_i^*. Consequently, $CEEC_i$ can elicit more funds amounting to c_i^* from the EU-15, as their bargaining power α_i increases.

---

[11] NB: The term 'bargaining power' is best understood as talent for negotiating or a player's skill in duping the other [151].

We recall that c_i^* is the share of costs of convergence C_i^C that is acceptable to the EU-15. With respect to the complete two-stage threat game $\Gamma(\varsigma_i, d)$ the NBS is, hence,

$$NBS : \Gamma^*(\varsigma_i, d) = (c_i^*, (1 - c_i)^* .$$

Considering the specific characteristics of the NBS, the combination of both players' Nash-strategies (('ERM II', 'overvalue'), 'give in') can also be represented in terms of their respective reaction functions R_{ij}. Due to complete information $CEEC_i$ can anticipate the EU-15's optimal choice, thus its own best response is:

$$R_{i1}(c_{i2}^*) = \begin{cases} 0 & \text{if } \dfrac{(1 + \lambda_i)\alpha_i - \beta_{-i}}{\alpha_i + \beta_{-i}} \le 0 \\ 0 < c_i \le 1 \text{ if } 0 < \dfrac{(1 + \lambda_i)\alpha_i - \beta_{-i}}{\alpha_i + \beta_{-i}} \le 1 \\ 1 & \text{else } \dfrac{(1 + \lambda_i)\alpha_i - \beta_{-i}}{\alpha_i + \beta_{-i}} > 1 \end{cases} \quad (5.13)$$

From the perspective of the EU-15 the corresponding reaction function is:

$$R_{i2}(c_{i1}^*) = \begin{cases} 0 & \text{if } \dfrac{2\beta_{-i} - \lambda_i\alpha_i}{\alpha_i + \beta_{-i}} \le 0 \\ 0 < (1 - c_i)^* \le 1 \text{ if } 0 < \dfrac{2\beta_{-i} - \lambda_i\alpha_i}{\alpha_i + \beta_{-i}} \le 1 \\ 1 & \text{else } \dfrac{2\beta_{-i} - \lambda_i\alpha_i}{\alpha_i + \beta_{-i}} > 1 \end{cases} \quad (5.14)$$

The players' reactions functions R_{ij} constitute the unique sub-game perfect Nash-equilibrium incorporating a specific NBS of the entire game $\Gamma(\varsigma_i, d)$ for every fixed $\bar{p} \,|\, \bar{p}^* \in P^*$ and $\bar{q} \,|\, \bar{q}^* \in Q^*$ (see (5.8) and (5.9)).

A special variation of the generalized NBS is the so-called symmetric (s)NBS. In respect to $\Gamma(\varsigma_i, d)$ the following simplification is made: The players' bargaining power the coefficients are fixed to $\alpha_i = \beta_{-i} = 0.5$.[12] In line with these considerations the reaction functions R_{ij} of the entire two-stage threat game $\Gamma(\varsigma_i, d)$ – i.e. for $CEEC_i$'s successful brinkmanship – can be reduced to

---

[12] When conceptualizing this symmetric NBS, Nash [150] himself had something like 'fair bargains' in mind. The particular discussion on whether only equally distributed bargaining power can be denoted as 'fair' is a broad topic. This debate is only of minor interest to our study, therefore, further discussion is omitted.

$$R_{i1}(c_{i2}^*) = \begin{cases} \frac{1}{2}\lambda_i & \text{if } 0 < \lambda_i < 1 \\ \frac{1}{2} & \text{if } \lambda_i = 1 \end{cases} \qquad (5.15)$$

and

$$R_{i2}(c_{i1}^*) = \begin{cases} 1 - \frac{1}{2}\lambda_i & \text{if } 0 < \lambda_i < 1 \\ \frac{1}{2} & \text{if } \lambda_i = 1 \end{cases}. \qquad (5.16)$$

If the cost structure in $\Gamma(\varsigma_i, d)$ allows $CEEC_i$ for enjoying the subsidiary role of the EU-15 to the full $(\lambda_i = 1)$[13] the ultimate bargaining outcome in view of the symmetric NBS is simply

$$symmetric\, NBS : \Gamma^*(\varsigma_i, d) = (\tfrac{1}{2}\lambda_i, 1 - \tfrac{1}{2}\lambda_i) = (\tfrac{1}{2}, \tfrac{1}{2}). \qquad (5.17)$$

This is to say, that both current and prospective members of the EMU split the costs of convergence equally – i.e. we agree with going 'fifty-fifty'. This handy, yet notable bargaining solution is confronted with the KSS in the following section.

5.2.2 Kalai-Smorodinsky Solution

This solution concept refers back to the work of Kalai and Smorodinsky [122]. The reasoning beyond the KSS is very different from the NBS. Although, the assumptions which apply to the NBS are also valid with regard to the KSS – i.e. complete information, common knowledge, and perfect commitment. Differences arise in terms of the specific axioms of monotonicity – which are still subject to a thorough debate – and the elimination of Nash's axiom for 'independence of irrelevant alternatives. Strictly speaking, this means the independence of alternatives other than the disagreement point d [173]. The KSS, however, makes use of an utopian ideal point (see below).

The motivation for the KSS is very much characterized by an idea of fairness. By the KSS, we pretend to grant both parties equal proportional concessions which are derived from its particular axiom of monotonicity. To motivate this players' mode of action we assume one player will have all the bargaining power. As with the NBS this would assign this player the best possible outcome and leave the other one empty handed – i.e. a take-it-or-leave-it offer would prevail. However,

---

[13] This is actually the rather ordinary case. The symmetric NBS has already been indicated in Figs. 5.5 and 5.1. In regard to the latter, this is the dashed 45°-line).

the idea is that if cooperative bargaining takes place the bargaining
solution should be a Pareto-optimal outcome where utilities are split
proportionally. This would most likely be the case where each player is
in the position of making a take-it-or-leave-it offer with the same probability. The KSS-concept seems applicable to our bargaining problem
when we presume that the envisaged negotiations are a 'nested game'
(see Sect. 2.2). If both players recognize that they will meet again –
whereas sometimes one player may have the upper hand, the other time
the other way round – they will probably act in line with this particular notion of fairness. The subsequent derivation of the KSS to our
maximization problem points to some more difficulties in applying the
KSS-concept to the bargaining game $\Gamma(\varsigma_i, d)$.

A graphical illustration of one possible KSS is portrayed in Fig. 5.6
which resembles the indicated bargaining outcome in Fig. 5.1 to a great
extent.

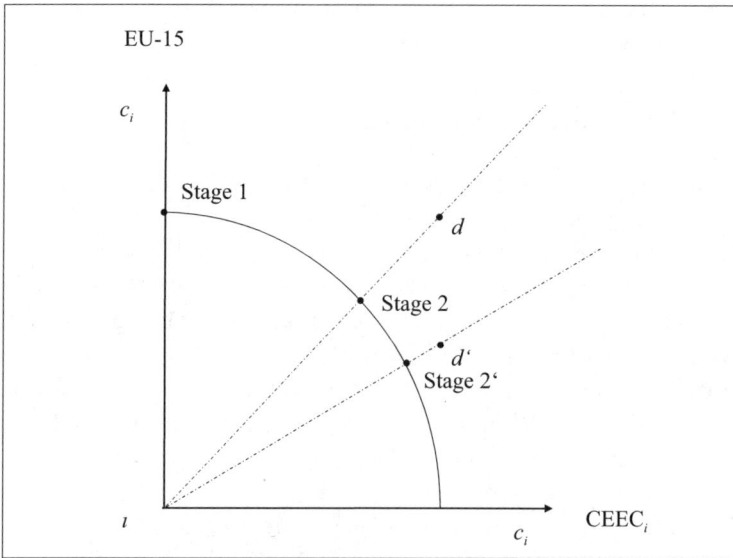

Fig. 5.6. Kalai-Smorodinsky solution

In particular, the KSS hinges upon the subsidiary role of the EU-
15. The maximization problem is basically the same the NBS-concept is
faced with; where each player's utility is specified in (5.2) and (5.3) (see
p. 86), and with $d = (-1, -\lambda_i)$. Furthermore, there is an utopian ideal

point $\iota_{(i)j} = (\iota_{i1}, \iota_2)$ which cannot be reached during the negotiations. The ideal point of both parties is to have no costs but certainly the benefits of completing the 'EU-enlargement' project. As the maximization problem is reduced to the cost argument, and is in line with previous simplifications of the bargaining game $\Gamma(\varsigma_i, d)$ the ideal point ι is the origin of the coordinate axes in Fig. 5.6. Therefore, the unattainable point $\iota_{(i)j} = (0, 0)$.

The KSS is the maximal point on the convex hull at the intersection with the line joining d to ι (see Fig. 5.6). For $c_{ij}^* \in \varsigma_i$ holds:[14]

$$\frac{(c_{i2}^* + \lambda_i)}{(c_{i1}^* + 1)} = \frac{(\iota_2 + \lambda_i)}{(\iota_{i1} + 1)}$$
$$\Rightarrow \frac{((1 - c_i) + \lambda_i)}{(c_i + 1)} = \frac{\lambda_i}{1} .$$

After rearranging we receive

$$c_i^* = \frac{1}{1 + \lambda_i}, \qquad 0 < \lambda_i \leq 1 . \tag{5.18}$$

This equilibrium outcome assigns $c_{i1}^* = c_i^*$ to a CEEC$_i$, whereas

$$c_{i2}^* = 1 - c_i^* = \frac{\lambda_i}{1 + \lambda_i}$$

is left to the EU-15.

Again, we can represent the players' reaction functions R_{ij} for the entire two-stage threat game $\Gamma(\varsigma, d)$ for every fixed $\bar{p} \,|\, \bar{p}^* \in P^*$ and $\bar{q} \,|\, \bar{q}^* \in Q^*$ (see (5.8) and (5.9)). The reactions functions are

$$R_{i1}(c_{i2}^*) = \begin{cases} \dfrac{1}{1 + \lambda_i} & \text{if } 0 < \lambda_i < 1 \\ \dfrac{1}{2} & \text{if } \lambda_i = 1 \end{cases} \tag{5.19}$$

and

$$R_{i2}(c_{i1}^*) = \begin{cases} \dfrac{\lambda_i}{1 + \lambda_i} & \text{if } 0 < \lambda_i < 1 \\ \dfrac{1}{2} & \text{if } \lambda_i = 1 \end{cases} . \tag{5.20}$$

---

[14] Actually, for an adequate representation of the KSS we would need to define another solution set and expand the feasible set respectively, particularly in regard to the axiom of monotonicity and the uniqueness of the solution. However, with respect to merely demonstrating the maximization problem this reduced form is sufficient.

The KSS for 'full subsidiarity' of the EU-15 is

$$KSS : \Gamma^*(\varsigma_i, d) = (\frac{1}{1 + \lambda_i}, \frac{\lambda_i}{1 + \lambda_i}) = (\frac{1}{2}, \frac{1}{2}) \, . \qquad (5.21)$$

These results are very counterintuitive: In cases with $0 < \lambda_i < 1$ –
i.e. which at $CEEC_i$ rather runs short of a deterrent threat deteriorating their brinkmanship – the EU-15 increases its assistance.[15] This
bargaining outcome is seemingly due to the 'utopian' monotonicity assumption of the KSS. Because a thorough investigation would get us
away from our subject matter, this puzzle is no longer tracked after.
Nonetheless, the other part of the solution for $\lambda_i = 1$ is very pleasant:
In cases where $CEEC_i$ is able to fully utilize the EU-15's willingness to
pay, the KSS coincides with the symmetric NBS in (5.17). To say it in
a few brief words: We would meet again halfway. However, the overall
impression is that the KSS-concept is hardly applicable to the fierce
bargaining on costs of convergence in ERM II.

Having thus far considered two cooperative bargaining solution concepts, non-cooperative concepts regain more attention in the next section.

5.2.3 Ståhl-Rubinstein Solution

In this section we apply a framework of infinite time horizons with
alternating offers to our game $\Gamma(\varsigma_i, d)$. The particular bargaining solution concept originates in the work of Ståhl [192], whose work has been
amended by Rubinstein [174]. The SRS is the most general and relevant of all bargaining solution concepts considered here. Additionally,
the SRS is a non-cooperative bargaining solution concept. This feature
distinguishes the SRS from the NBS and the KSS. Most notably, its
non-cooperative characteristic brings the SRS close to our understanding of the two-stage threat game. In regard to the brinkmanship game,
an advantage of the SRS is that the subsequent haggling about the
distribution of the costs of convergence gains more prominence. This
is taking into account that the duration of negotiating affects markets
calculus, i.e. the mechanism of punishing in this game. The latter is
quite realistic: The longer the negotiations take, the more it becomes
obvious from the perspective of markets that both parties are unable
or unwilling to agree on a $CEEC_i$'s appropriate policy mix in ERM II –
i.e. basically fiscal policy as monetary policy is brought to a standstill

---

[15] Figure 5.6, for instance, at which the equilibrium moves to the intersection with
the line joining d' to the coordinate axes at the point Stage 2' depicts such oddity.

in the context of high capital mobility. Both players are well-aware that time is not on their side. Contrary to the general association of the SRS as a 'shrinking pie' (i.e. utility) over time, here the 'pie of costs' inflates over time and will leave its mark on both parties upon collapsing – i.e. both are incurred with costs of default. For that reason, the SRS makes use of players' 'patience', so that despite an infinite horizon the imped-ing risk of a breakdown makes both parties agree on the distribution of the costs of convergence in finite time. Accordingly, the settlement of the bargaining is especially dependent on each players' negotiating skills, which are modelled here in terms of 'patience'.[16]

The following Fig. 5.7 depicts the SRS for our bargaining on costs of convergence.

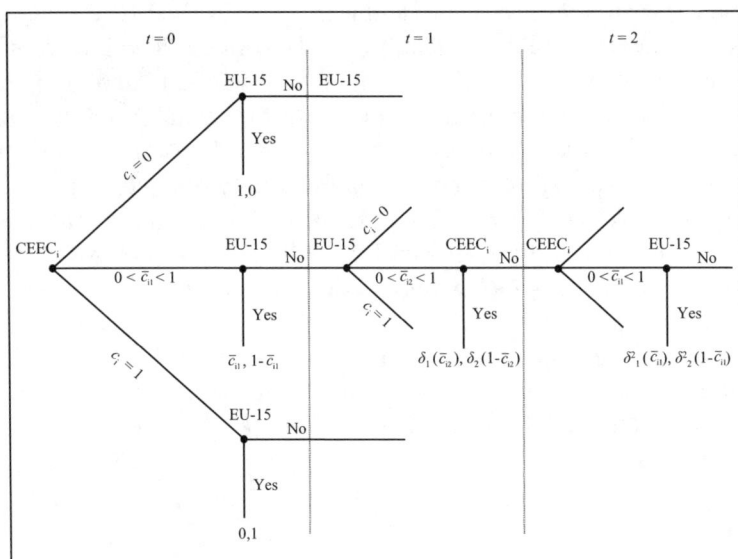

Fig. 5.7. Ståhl-Rubinstein's alternating offers

As in the cases of the NBS and the KSS the players are well-informed – i.e. the assumptions of complete information and common knowledge apply to the SRS. The negotiations proceed as follows: At the outset of their brinkmanship – i.e. $CEEC_i$ pursue a 'threaten-thy-neighbour'-policy – the $CEEC_i$ makes a particular offer in $t = 0$. This offer con-

_____

[16] As is the case with poker, the player who can longer convincingly conceal his fear of being faced with the costs of a negotiations breakdown is better off.

sists of demanding financial assistance amounting to $\bar{c}_{i2}$ (again, with $0 \le c_{ij} \le 1$, $c_{ij} \in \varsigma_i$, $\varsigma_i \subset \mathbb{R}^2$) sufficient to keep CEEC$_i$ from further brinkmanship. The EU-15 can accept – i.e. choosing "Yes" – or refuse – i.e. choosing "No" (see Fig. 5.7). When the EU-15 rejects the offer, it can make an counter-offer $\bar{c}_{i2}$ in $t = \tau$ whereas τ denotes the length of the interval between two successive offers (for reasons of convenience, the interval is for the time being normalized to $\tau = 1, 2, ..., \infty$ as in Fig. 5.7). In turn, CEEC$_i$ can refuse or accept. As no player refuses once and for all – in that case the outcome would be the disagreement point d – but makes counter-offers, the bargaining is infinite. However, the SRS-concept requires amending the original players' utility functions to $u_j(c_i, t) = v_j(c_i)\delta_{(i)j}^t$ where $\delta_{(i)j}$ is a player's time-preference.[17] In line with previous considerations $u_{(i)j}(0, t) = 0$, $u_{(i)j}(1, 0) = 0$, and $\lim_{t \to \infty} u_{(i)j}(c_{ij}, t) = 0$ when the game would go on forever.

Stationary strategies are of particular interest to the SRS. Strategies are stationary when a player's history is of no interest. That is every player j always plans to make the same offer – which is here a specific share $\bar{c}_{ij}$ of costs of convergence – every second round regardless of any previously rejected offers and counter-offers. Only an equilibrium offer makes the responding player indifferent between refusing ("No") and accepting ("Yes") (see Fig. 5.7). Because of stationary strategies – indicated by the double-lines in Fig. 5.8 – CEEC$_i$ always offers a cost-sharing deal $k = (\bar{c}_{i1}, 1 - \bar{c}_{i1})$, whereas the EU-15 always proposes the deal $l = (\bar{c}_{i2}, 1 - \bar{c}_{i2})$.

At the same time, the EU-15 always accepts an offer k (or anything better) and rejects anything worse, whereas the same goes for CEEC$_i$ as regards the offer l. The offers are represented by the vectors $\mathbf{a} = u_{(i)j}(k, t)$ and $\mathbf{b} = u_{(i)j}(l, t)$. For instance, $a_2 = u_2(k, 2) = u_2((1 - \bar{c}_{i1}), 1) = v_2(1 - \bar{c}_{i1})\delta_2^2$ would be the EU-15's pay-off when accepting the CEEC$_i$'s counter-offer at time $t = 2$ as portrayed in Fig. 5.7. Since the SRS assumes common knowledge and perfect foresight backward induction is allowed. This is to say that both players anticipate the final bargaining outcome in the first round. The alternating offer framework reduces, thus, to Fig. 5.8. Generally, in equilibrium the players are indifferent between accepting and rejecting, so that for every arbitrary interval τ between alternating offers

---

[17] Similar to risk-preferences, time-preferences $\delta_{(i)j}$ affect pay-offs. However, the latter is a way of modelling 'patience' and negotiating skills respectively, whereas the former directly affect the players' attitudes towards the pay-offs.

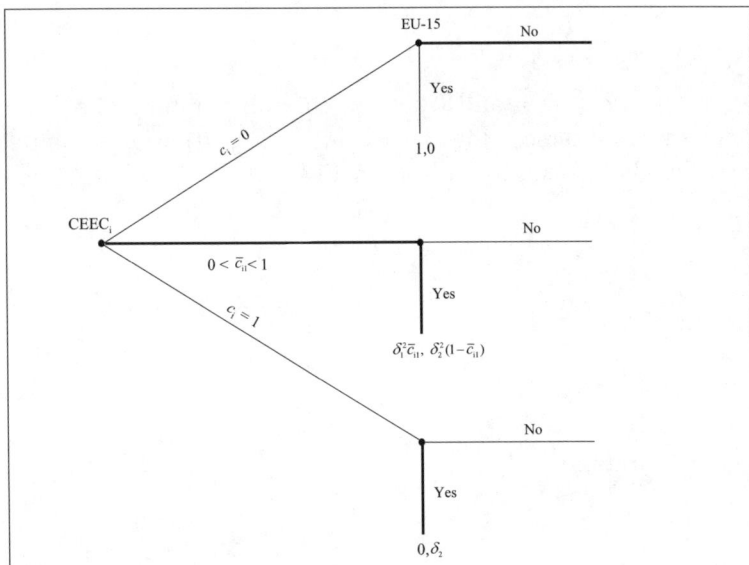

Fig. 5.8. Ståhl-Rubinstein's alternating offers with backward induction

$$a_2 = \delta_2^\tau b_2 \text{ and} \tag{5.22}$$
$$b_1 = \delta_{i1}^\tau a_1 . \tag{5.23}$$

Another transformation is necessary in order to show that there is a stationary sub-game perfect equilibrium: In (5.22) and (5.23) we replace the discount rates by $\delta_{(i)j} = e^{-\varrho_{(i)j}}$, with $\varrho_{(i)j}$ as the players' instantaneous rate of interest and time-preferences rates respectively. In that way, we obtain

$$a_2 = e^{-\varrho_2 \tau} b_2 \text{ and} \tag{5.24}$$
$$b_1 = e^{-\varrho_{i1} \tau} a_1 . \tag{5.25}$$

The time-preferences rates $\varrho_{(i)j}$ are inversely proportional to our bargaining power coefficients α_i and β_{-i} (see p. 78). Obviously, this is due to the fact that 'impatience' deteriorates a player's bargaining power. Therefore, we can also write $\alpha_i = \frac{1}{\varrho_{i1}}$ and $\beta_{-i} = \frac{1}{\varrho_2}$. From (5.24) and (5.25) it follows that

$$\left(\frac{a_2}{b_2}\right)^\beta_{-i} = \left(\frac{b_1}{a_1}\right)^\alpha_i = e^{-\tau} . \tag{5.26}$$

This, in turn, implies that

$$a_1^{\alpha_i} a_2^{\beta_{-i}} = b_1^{\alpha_i} b_2^{\beta_{-i}} \ .$$

Accordingly, the vectors **a** and **b** are on the same hyperbola. Though, this hyperbola can intersect the convex hull of $\Gamma(\varsigma_i, d)$ at any point such as depicted by the broken hyperbola in Fig. 5.9.

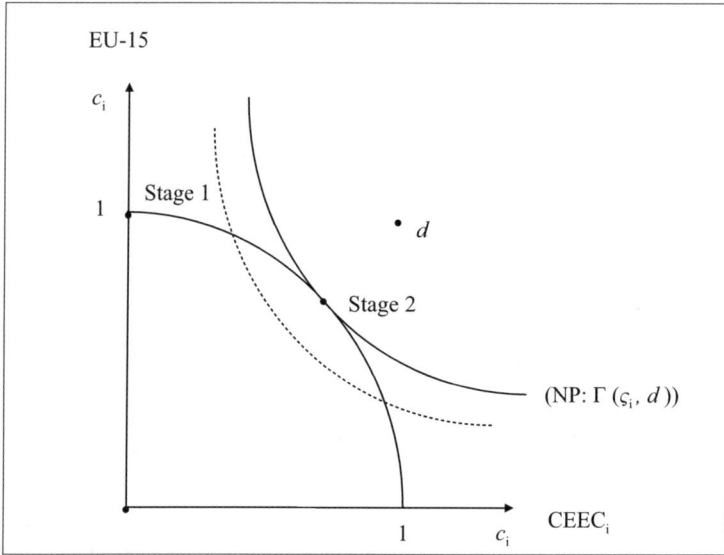

Fig. 5.9. Ståhl-Rubinstein solution

The SRS has the advantage that it converges on the NBS for intervals $\tau \to 0$, i.e. that **a** and **b** converge on the same value [22]. This is the case for the hyperbola – corresponding to our Nash-product of $\Gamma(\varsigma_i, d)$ in (5.10) – which is tangent to the convex hull in the equilibrium of stage 2 in Fig. 5.9. In order to demonstrate that the SRS eventually coincides with the NBS it has to be shown that the hyperbola has a tangential point with the convex hull [22]. For $\tau \to 0$ it follows that

$$\lim_{\tau \to 0} e^{-\tau} = 1.$$

Accordingly, it holds true that

$$\lim_{\tau \to 0} \left(\frac{a_2}{b_2} \right)^{\beta} = \lim_{\tau \to 0} \left(\frac{b_1}{a_1} \right)^{\alpha} = 1 \ ,$$

so that

$$a_2 = b_2 \quad \text{and} \quad a_1 = b_1 \; .$$

Transforming these into each players' initial offer yields

$$\bar{c}_{i1} = \bar{c}_{i2} \; .$$

This is to say, that both players' offers correspond to each other for $\tau \to 0$, thus, the convex hull and the hyperbola (NP) have a tangential point constituting a unique bargaining outcome. This result is highly plausible against the background of assuming that there exist well-informed players $CEEC_i$ and EU-15, who are familiar with each respective risk-attitude and talent for negotiating. In addition, assuming that the sword of Damocles – i.e. increasing negotiation time precipitates a speculative attack – hangs over the bargaining players calls for presuming $\tau \to 0$. Therefore, the non-cooperative SRS-concept with its specific equilibrium at the Pareto frontier of ς_i is a proper representation of the bargaining over costs of convergence in ERM II.

Regarding our maximization problem, the SRS-concept produces exactly the same bargaining outcome as the NBS. This is valid in regard to $\tau \to 0$, which is of particular interest to our brinkmanship game. The equilibrium offers a result in the same unique bargaining solution c_i^* for the entire two-stage threat game $\Gamma(\varsigma_i, d)$ as in (5.12). The same applies to the players' reactions functions $R_{(i)j}$ in (5.13) and (5.14) – or (5.15) and (5.16) for the symmetric NBS.

   Moreover, if we again assume that 'patience' and the talent for negotiating respectively as well as players' risk-preferences are neutral, than the haggling about sharing the costs of convergence results in the symmetric NBS (see (5.17)). Certainly, the SRS also corresponds to the KSS (see (5.21)) when $CEEC_i$ can fully utilize the limited liability ($\lambda_i = 1$) of the EU-15.

5.3 Results

In this section, we have examined the CEECs' brinkmanship in ERM II, more generally, in transitory fixed exchange-rate arrangements of the EU-enlargement processes. In doing so, we have developed a two-player game. It has been shown that designing a two-player constellation is not only a necessary concession in respect of creating a minimal common denominator for the various bargaining-solution concepts. On the contrary, this course of action is highly plausible give the competition among all CEECs on the run for EU-15's financial assistance. It has been shown that a single $CEEC_i$ can be in a position to threaten to halt the entire enlargement process under identifiable conditions. These conditions are, firstly, the likelihood of effectively infuriating voters by adhering to Maastricht criteria and, secondly, the probability of encountering a frugal EU when a $CEEC_i$ practises the 'threaten-thy-neighbour' strategy. Regarding the latter, the according probability p denotes the EU-15's ability to parry CEECs' claims in any sphere of European decision-making, particulary with regard to European structural policies. The probability q_i, however, links the potential voter alienation in the course of Maastricht compliance – possibly spoiling the entire European integration process – with the 'Obstfeld' trade-off in currency-crisis models.

Passing through ERM II has been represented as a two-stage threat game with a possible unique subgame-perfect equilibrium for the strategies (('ERM II', 'overvalue'), 'give in'). The game G reflects the final investment phase of completing the 'EU-enlargement' project, which ensures the provision of the public good 'political stability' in CEE. Because of this game's particular feature of being a strictly competitive zero sum game we have transformed the two-stage threat game to $\Gamma(\varsigma_i, d)$. The corresponding standardization of costs and benefits facilitated the subsequent analysis of the bargaining on costs of convergence.

In search of a unique Nash equilibrium of the two-stage threat game, we investigated the NBS, the KSS, and the SRS. The rationale of this course of action – in line with the Nash programme – has been to reveal a robust bargaining solution. Every bargaining-solution concept incorporates different aspects of the negotiation. We have formulated the a general bargaining solution, which also takes the specific subsidiary role of the EU-15 into account. In this context, it has been shown that the KSS may be exotic. This is to say that it may generate bargaining outcomes, at which is valid that a weaker a $CEEC_i$, the higher the financial assistance. This result is 'too fair' for appropriately portraying the bargaining situation of EU-15 and a single $CEEC_i$. Henceforth, we attach only minor importance to the KSS. However, the NBS, the KSS, and the SRS converge on a unique bargaining outcome particularly in the case of identical neutral risk preferences and bargaining powers among the players and a $CEEC_i$ that is enable to fully utilize the limited liability of EU-15. This specific bargaining outcome is depicted by the simplest version of the symmetric NBS (see (5.17)). The players' reactions functions $R_{(i)j}$ representing Nash strategies of our two-stage threat game for every $\bar{p} \,|\, \bar{p}^* \in P^*$ and $\bar{q} \,|\, \bar{q}^* \in Q^*$ (see (5.8) and (5.9)) resolve our maximization problem.

Summarily, the EU-15 most probably pays CEECs for implementing the right exchange-rate policies – i.e. we probably agree to a 'fifty-fifty' split when redistributing the costs of convergence. In the following, we highlight which CEECs are eligible for brinkmanship against the EU-15.

6

Empirical Analysis

In the following analysis, we sketch how our model can be examined empirically. The subsequent empirical analysis results in a stylized political forecast of each $CEEC_i$'s brinkmanship probability and the involved costs. We consider an EMU-accession scenario, in which all CEECs enter ERM II at the same time in 2005. In this context, we distinguish between a baseline, optimistic, and pessimistic scenario regarding the estimated costs of convergence. The availability of reliable data restricts the quality of this empirical examination. We estimate the stochastic cost parameters – i.e. the costs of default C_i^D and the Maastricht costs of convergence C_i^C on the basis of a data sample that includes estimates and forecasts from the period 1993–2009. These parameters affect the effectiveness and acceptability conditions of the brinkmanship. We compute the bounds of the threat game with the help of a Monte-Carlo simulation. In addition, the crucial probabilities q_i and p are predicted: Searching for a suitable proxy for q_i, we conduct some binomial logit regressions in order to estimate the propensity of increasing EU-aversion due to rising unemployment in the course of passing through ERM II. This way, the empirical examination projects the country-specific sensitivity of voter demand for the public good "exchange-rate policy". The derived measure is a proxy of the probability q_i of shifts in exchange-rate policy triggering currency crises and spreading defaults. Unfortunately, the employed data do not allow for significant estimations. Nonetheless, some further restrictions enable the use of a much simpler proxy for the country-specific capacities of political clout against European integration within the constituency. Additionally, the probability p denotes the likelihood of encountering a frugal EU-15, when a $CEEC_i$ is practising brinkmanship. We argue that a Banzhaf-power index is a suitable approximation. The current members' remaining influence in legislative EU-decision making after the admittance of ten new members represents the probability p.

Having dealt with the estimations of cost parameters (Sect. 6.1) and proxies for potential voter alienation and EU-aversion respectively (Sect. 6.2), as well as the EU-15's ability to deter new members' claims (Sect. 6.3), a Monte-Carlo simulation of the stochastic bounds of brinkmanship (Sect. 6.4) completes empirical analysis. Finally, the simulation results for a CEECs' brinkmanship and the costs involved are summarized (Sect. 6.5). According to the stylized empirical model the three Baltic countries Estonia, Latvia, and Lithuania, as well as Hungary are eligible candidates for brinkmanship. This is to say, that these countries will experience costs of convergence in ERM II with which they can successfully burden current members of the EMU with.

6.1 Estimations of Cost Parameters

Until now, the study has argued that the bargaining in ERM II revolves around the Maastricht costs of convergence in conjunction with a deterrent threat that is based on provoking costs of default. In this regard, it is quite useful to compare the subsequent calculations with other estimations in the literature for the costs attributed to the entire EU-enlargement process. In this manner, we obtain an appreciation of the importance of the threat game to the costs of European eastward enlargement. To put it bluntly, we get an impression as to whether effective cost bargaining will grant the CEECs the shirt off the current EMU-members' back, or whether these costs are rather marginal.

Baldwin, Francois, and Portes [13] consider some different budget scenarios for EU-enlargement costs for current EU members. The estimated long-term net costs of EU-enlargement amount to about 0.01% of the EU-15's GDP [13]. These authors take into account possible integration effects such as trade effects, Single Market effects, factor movements etc. Dicke and Foders [63] overview and update some estimates for the additional fiscal costs cropping up in the course of the European eastward enlargement process. Such fiscal costs in the EU-budget are of particular interest to our study. These authors suppose that the increase in the EU-budget ranges from 13–37.2 bn. Euro per annum after the EU-enlargement [63].[1] The predicted brinkmanship game costs are subsequently compared with the aforementioned estimations.

---

[1] In accordance with the 'Adjustment of the financial framework 2000–06 for enlargement' these estimates are in prices from 1999.

6.1.1 Costs of Default

With regard to the costs of default C_i^D relevant expectation values are available. According studies refer to past experiences with exchange-rate crises. We follow Bordo et al. [31] when estimating C_i^D in terms of output loss, i.e. a currency crisis' depth. These authors measure output loss as the cumulative differences between pre-crisis trend growth and actual growth. In this context, the same authors deploy an indicator to spot a currency crisis. According to their perspective, an exchange-rate crisis is present when there is a change spotted in parity, a relinquishment of a fixed exchange-rate regime, an international bailout, or considerable exchange market pressure. In respect of exchange market pressure, these authors make use of an index, which comprises a weighted average of exchange-rate change, short-term interest-rate change, and reserve change relative to the centre country [31].

In regard to CEECs it is acceptable to treat these countries like emerging-market countries. Similar to the latter CEECs receive sizable capital inflows in an economic environment that is characterized by high capital mobility. Eichengreen and Bordo [72] use a sample comprised of 56 emerging-market countries during the period of 1973–97. The group of emerging-market countries experienced an average output loss amounting to 7.00% GDP [72]; this expectation value is normally distributed with a standard deviation of 8.23% GDP. Such loss is, on average, regained within about two year's time, more precisely, within 2.09 years [72]. Moreover, the same authors calculate the average output loss in countries which undergo a currency crisis and a banking crisis. In such a case, the costs of default amount to 19.46% GDP in the average, whereas recovery takes almost 3.5 years [72]. However, we restrict our analysis to the rather less disastrous case of a simple exchange-rate crisis. Hence, about half of the average output loss serves as an expectation value for our costs of default. Though, this values is rather underestimated as the two years of economic recovery usually take on a J-curve course – i.e. the trough of economic slack falls into the first year.[2] Nonetheless, without exception we estimate the yearly average output loss (in terms of % GDP) for a CEEC$_i$ experiencing a currency crisis at $C_i^D = C^D$, $C^D \sim N(\mu^D, (\sigma^D)^2)$ with $\mu^D = -3.3$ and $\sigma^D = 5.7$. These estimates are compared with the relative Maastricht costs of convergence.

---

[2] Unfortunately, the according data have not been available.

6.1.2 Costs of Convergence

There is a tug-of-war over the distribution of the Maastricht costs of convergence in ERM II. These costs of convergence arise in terms of an output gap (see the discussion in Sect. 3.3). However, forecasts of output gap are rare and only partly reliable. The fundamental rationale of output-gap estimates, is that there is a potential level of economic activity that can be achieved given the economic resources available at any particular point in time. Output gap is the difference between potential and actual output. Positive values point to over-utilization of production inputs in the economy, while negative values indicate excess capacities. The latter usually refers to a labour force that is not being used to full capacity, leaving some level of unemployment in the economy. Theoretical and statistical approaches are quoted for estimations of trend real GDP growth rates [171]. The theoretical approach makes use of so-called production function methods. Such approaches employ a country-specific Cobb-Douglas production function. In order to estimate an approximate production function, information is required about the amounts of capital and labour used in production. Although data on labour forces are often accurate, statistics about capital stocks are rare and difficult to approximate. This applies particularly to economies in CEE [81]. The statistical approach, in particular the Hodrick–Prescott (HP)-filter, is often used when relevant data for a production function method are not available. This HP-filter encompasses an adjustment rule, at which the trend component moves continuously and adjusts gradually. This statistical method has the advantage of being easy to apply. The only data that is needed is a time series of actual output or real growth rates. The other side of the coin is that according forecasts often produce sobering estimates. This is due to the fact that the HP-filter is not linked to economic theory, but a pure statistical device. In addition, it is valid that the smaller the economy – for instance, such as the Baltic countries, – the greater the impact of exogenous shocks and of exchange rates on output (see p. 52); thereby, worsening the forecasts for such countries. Moreover, there is a general objection to both lines of approaches: If output gap stems from disinflation policy, then estimates may ignore the possibly positive impact on growth [153]. However, CEECs have already made considerable progress in disinflation and reduced their inflation to a level which is – at least to some extent – already close to the inflation level in the eurozone (see Table 4.1 on p. 60).We, therefore, presume that additional disinflation shows without exception a negative impact on growth prospects and output level.

We distinguish between baseline (B), optimistic (O), and pessimistic (P) scenarios. The alternatives to the baseline scenario consider a 50% alteration of input value – i.e. the costs of convergence are eased and aggravated respectively. The estimates of costs of convergence in for the CEECs for our reference year of 2005 are summarized in Table 6.1.[3]

Table 6.1. Estimated costs of convergence for the year 2005

	CZ	EST	HUN	LAT	LIT	PL	SLK	SLO
i	1	2	3	4	5	6	7	8
B μ_i^C	0,3	-0,4	-0,5	-1,0	-0,2	0,5	0,2	0,4
O μ_i^C	0,45	-0,2	-0,25	-0,5	-0,1	0,75	0,3	0,6
P μ_i^C	0,15	-0,6	-0,75	-1,5	-0,3	0,25	0,1	0,2

Regarding standard deviations we calculate a single average standard deviation of estimated output gaps on the basis of these IMF real GDP growth rate forecasts for eight CEECs. This is to say that we repeatedly subtract the current residual component of HP-filtering from the same projected and forecasted values of the previous year and the year before that. In this way, we obtain a mean value of 'forecast errors' which represent all standard deviations σ_i^C of costs of convergence.

When generating deviations I have utilized a maximum lag of two-years forward. A recourse to even earlier years would weaken the accuracy of the estimations. In this context, we have to reject the normal distribution assumption for these estimated residuals: A skewness-kurtosis test indicates that this assumption cannot be maintained at any reasonable conventional level of significance. A change in the selection of comparison years does not further ameliorate the estimates. In lieu of a better estimator we draw on a $\sigma_i^C = 1.35$. Given our relatively small estimates for output gaps (μ_i^C) the variation is rather steep.

Some information about the validity of our estimates can be provided by comparing the same values with the Maastricht costs of convergence incurred during 1995–97. In this regard, the inclusion of countries which have been deemed economic laggards – i.e. a smaller GDP per capita than the respective average of the founding EMU-members

---

[3] The calculations are based on using a HP-filter for estimating output gap (% GDP) from a series of annual real GDP growth rates from 1993–2009. Applying a production function method would be out of proportion to the results of our study. Data are taken from various IMF Country Reports for the years 2000–04. Previous data, which are not displayed within IMF country reports, have been taken from the IMF's World Economic Outlook [117, 118].

– is also necessary. Correspondingly, it is assumed that these countries had to pass through a catching-up phase which was curtailed by mandatory Maastricht criteria. Finland, Ireland, Italy, Portugal, and Spain experienced such output gaps.

Table 6.2. Output gaps in EU-member countries 1995–97

	1995	1996	1997
Finland	-7,0	-5,6	-2,8
Ireland	-1,9	-1,5	1,2
Italy	-1,0	-1,5	-1,1
Portugal	-1,3	-0,2	0,7
Spain	-4,0	-4,4	-3,2

The values lie within a range of -7.0% GDP for Finland in 1995 and a positive output gap of 1.2% GDP of excess capacities in Ireland in 1997 (see Table 6.2).[4] Admittedly, not all of these output gaps are due to Maastricht. Instead, the impact of the EMS-crisis 1992–93 becomes noticeable here. This applies particularly to Finland. However, even the year 1997 demonstrates output gaps ranging between -3.2% GDP in Spain to the mentioned 1.2% GDP in Ireland. Accordingly, comparing these data conveys the impression that our expected costs of convergence $C_i^C, C_i^C \sim N(\mu_i^C, \sigma_i^C)$ are on no account exaggerated, but lie within normal ranges of output gaps. Thus, these estimates are to some extent reliable, and they provide a reasonable clue for our stylized political forecast.

6.2 Estimations of EU-Aversion

Estimations on both the probabilities q_i and p gain more prominence in this section. The former captures the likelihood of triggering an exchange-rate crisis. For given parameters of C_i^C and C^D the probability q_i provides information on whether a $CEEC_i$'s brinkmanship satisfies the effectiveness condition. At the same time, p denotes the probability that the EU-15 can withstand the prospective EMU-members' demand for the provision of additional financial transfers toward the CEECs. In turn, p affects the acceptability condition of a $CEEC_i$'s 'threaten-thy-neighbour' strategy.

---

[4] Data (in % GDP) are taken from [157]

Regarding q_i, we try our hand at a binomial logit analysis in hopes of finding the most appropriate proxy for q_i in this procedure. For this purpose, we make use of the Central and Eastern Eurobarometer (CEEB) [48]. The CEEB provides the latest disaggregated data for voters' EU-aversion and expectations regarding future employment prospects. However, there are serious setbacks in an empirical analysis of predicted country-specific probabilities q_i. This is due to the fact, that the selected country sample does not allow for a sound estimation. Therefore, we refer to the aggregated data of the Candidate Countries Eurobarometer (CCEB) [47]. This way, we gain a rough proxy for the country-specific potential of infuriated electorates opposing European integration thereby, triggering a speculative attack.

Estimating q_i for potential voter alienation on account of undesirable costs of convergence is challenging. Basically, we strive for a proxy for the likelihood of infuriated voters coercing a government to change policy supply. Such shift in policy may then precipitate a reversal of capital flows, as a result of which a currency crisis ensues. Consequently, the investment project 'EU enlargement' would be obstructed – i.e. the provision of the public good 'political stability' in CEE would deteriorate.

In accordance with our political-economic framework in Chap. 2, we suppose that if portions of the electorate become unemployed during the Maastricht qualification process, these specific voters will reduce their supply of public approval. The public will oppose the government's track of economic policy in respect of an existing fixed exchange-rate regime. In this situation, incumbent politicians may be forced to back down – i.e. to compensate such 'losers' of the European integration process. This relative change in EU-aversion acts as a 'stimulus' within the political system. The greater the stimulus, the greater the likelihood that a government will respond to the according demand and will alter the status quo of exchange-rate policy, thus, undermining the credibility of the soft peg.

In line with the two-level metaphor, national executives play the hardships of voter alienation off against current EMU-members. On the intergovernmental level, the CEECs' governments may pass on their voters' propensity to offend European integration depending on falling from the group of employed people into the group of the jobless in an undistorted manner. In doing so, national executives fully utilize increasing EU-aversion when bargaining over the costs of convergence with the EU-15.

A binomial logit analysis can be of great help in capturing the marginal propensity of electorates voting against EMU-membership and general European integration matters. In this respect, we attempt to predict the probability of EMU-membership opposition in relation to aggravating unemployment levels. We, therefore, conduct a simple binomial logit analysis. In some respects, such analysis leaves the absolute level of voting against European integration – i.e. the level of EU-aversion – unaccounted for. Instead, it measures marginal effects, which here correspond to the probabilities of change in EU-aversion. In particular, changes in EU-aversion occurring after CEECs' admittance to the EU act as new stimuli within a political system. Hence, marginal effects are of special relevance. A common procedure is to evaluate such sensitivities at the mean, which is substituted here by the frequency of each categorized occupational group. The empirical analysis relies upon data from the CEEB 1997.[5] This survey covers about 1000 respondents taken from our eight candidate CEECs, plus Bulgaria and Romania.

EU-aversion, in terms of opposing European integration and EMU-membership respectively, is approximated by the group "temporarily not working, unemployed" – which is denoted as "jobless" (see Table 6.3) – choosing "vote against Membership". Accordingly, this categorial variable is recorded by individual answers to the question: "If there were to be a referendum on the question of (OUR COUNTRY'S) membership of the European Union, would you personally vote for or against membership?". Respondents in the sample are initially grouped into five categories: 'Vote for membership', 'Vote against membership', 'Undecided', 'Would not vote', and 'Don't know/ no answer'. We condense these into two groups – i.e. 'Vote against membership' is recoded as a 1 and other answers are coded as a 0. For control variables, we include age, education, income and other subgroups of 'occupation of respondent'.[6] The intuitive expectation is that respondents becoming jobless are more likely to exhibit EU-aversion. Table 6.3 displays the according empirical findings.[7]

---

[5] At the moment, this is the latest available decomposed opinion poll. The entire Central Eastern Eurobarometer (CEEB) 1990–97 is already put into individual components. The period of 1998–2000 is not covered by any poll, although there is the Candidate Countries Eurobarometer (CCEB), which was set up in 2001. Unfortunately, the according queries are often not that compatible with the CCEB. As of now, disaggregated data from these polls has not been available.

[6] The latter are included as a series of dummy variables, whereas 'civil servants' are excluded.

[7] Intercepts and categorial variables for other occupations are not reported. The dependent variable is 'hypothetically voting against EU membership in 1997'.

Table 6.3. Results of binomial logit analysis

Pooled obs.: 10349		Age	Education	Income	Jobless
	B	0,008*	-0,389***	-0,077***	0,602**
	S.E.	0,004	0,046	0,012	0,259

Czech Republic obs.: 967		Age	Education	Income	Jobless
	B	0,003	-0,486***	-0,038	0,306
	S.E.	0,014	0,185	0,044	0,975

Estonia obs.: 1007		Age	Education	Income	Jobless
	B	0,024	-0,075	-0,011	1,622
	S.E.	0,020	0,210	0,072	1,221

Hungary obs.: 1080		Age	Education	Income	Jobless
	B	0,027**	-0,495***	-0,078	0,202
	S.E.	0,013	0,186	0,079	0,695

Latvia obs.: 1025		Age	Education	Income	Jobless
	B	-0,010	-0,324**	-0,018	1,104
	S.E.	0,013	0,150	0,049	1,092

Lithuania obs.: 1013		Age	Education	Income	Jobless
	B	-0,012	-0,555***	-0,034	0,328
	S.E.	0,010	0,140	0,036	0,699

Poland obs.: 997		Age	Education	Income	Jobless
	B	0,016	-0,661***	-0,030	-0,076
	S.E.	0,014	0,201	0,045	1,212

Slovakia obs.: 997		Age	Education	Income	Jobless
	B	0,005	-0,592	-0,023	0,948
	S.E.	0,017	0,249	0,057	0,884

Slovenia obs.: 1042		Age	Education	Income	Jobless
	B	-0,015	-0,300*	-0,106*	0,309
	S.E.	0,014	0,174	0,054	0,798

A natural starting point takes a look at a single pooled data set. Coefficients and standard errors from the analysis of the pooled sample are depicted in the first row of Table 6.3. The supposed relation between the group 'jobless' and increasing EU-aversion is weakly significant. The controls show that EU-aversion grows as age increases and declines with higher income and education levels.

We estimate the marginal effects by putting all the explanatory variables to their sample means. Accordingly, the relevant marginal effect for EU-aversion of respondents becoming jobless, evaluated at the mean, is 0.036. This implies that a one point increase in the 'jobless' group would increase a country's probability of voter alienation with respect to opposing the European integration process by 3.6%. However, when studying the single pooled data set this is a general effect, which may outweigh country-by-country variation. This is why we are particularly interested in country-specific values of q_i. At this stage we face the adversity that none of the values for country-by-country differentiated groups of 'jobless' are significant (see the last column of Table 6.3).[8] The most probable reason is that very few people who have fallen into the 'jobless' category are likely to respond to such a survey – the according quota ranges from 2,7% to about 10% of all respondents.[9] Therefore, this binomial-logit analysis is of no further help – i.e. this portion of the empirical examination fails to bring out the probabilities of q_i in this manner.

This problem occurs in related literature, as well. Tucker, Pacek, and Berinsky [203] conduct a comprehensive multi-nomial logit analysis in order to predict the probability of support for EU-membership.[10] These authors distinguish between self-defined 'winners' and 'losers' – further differentiated in terms of supporters and adversaries of free-market economies – which they divide into four (instead of our two) groups. Their results for the group of 'temporarily not working, unem-

---

Levels of significance: Sig. *** $< 0,01$, Sig. ** $< 0,05$, Sig. * $< 0,1$. NB: The pooled sample also comprises data for Bulgaria and Romania.

[8] In this context, Poland represents an interesting outlier in the sample as the sign of the coefficient indicates that apparently even the presumed relation between becoming 'jobless' and EU-aversion seems invalid.

[9] In this regard, the Czech Republic represents the lowest bound with 20 of 739 selected cases included in the analysis, whereas Latvia constitutes the upper bound with 93 out of 927 cases.

[10] Their according support values are not applicable with respect to our problem. Besides, we have given precedence to a simple binomial logit instead of a multi-nomial logit analysis. This is due to the fact that a multi-nomial expenditure would be out of proportion to the results and beyond the ambitions of this stylized political forecast.

ployed' are also insignificant [203]. Hence, we consider an alternative proxy.

For lack of a better proxy, we construct a simpler measure for the probability q_i. For this purpose, we need an auxiliary argument. Until now, the line of argument has been to suppose that the change in EU-aversion instead of its absolute level is the most appropriate proxy for q_i. The rationale is that eventually only an increase in the level of EU-aversion in CEECs after their admittance to the EU gains political clout in a way which affects political decision-making. Different levels of EU-aversion are only of secondary interest, for instance, because these have been of minor importance with regard to fixing a joint date for CEECs receiving EU-membership status. Various compensation payments and modifications of policy supplies in the domestic arena may have calmed EU-aversion among the constituencies. In this exact way, the auxiliary argument takes effect: Prior to the CEECs' EU accession, the level of evident EU-aversion has been of minor importance as these countries have excelled at good conduct. Albeit, analogously to the rationale of the weighing-in-syndrome (see p. 72), CEECs may refrain from further immediate compensation for 'losers' and adversaries in their European integration process. Instead of this, these governments play up the potential of corresponding voter alienation against current members of the EMU.[11]

In accordance with this line of argument, the effective share of EU-membership is 'a bad thing' relative to 'a good thing' and 'neither good nor bad', and leaving aside respondents that choose 'don't know/ no answer' is a suitable proxy q_i. Table 6.4 displays the relevant data taken from the CCEB 2001.1–2004.1.

The relevant query in the CCEB is "Generally speaking, do you think that (COUNTRY)'s membership of the European Union would be...?". The level of EU-aversion is the highest in Latvia with an average of $\mu_4^q = 0,18$, whereas Slovakia shows the lowest level with an average of $\mu_7^q = 0,06$. A caveat is that the Eurobarometer data exhibit some volatility as reflected in σ_i^q. However, the sample is too small for dismantling a trend component for a more sophisticated estimate of μ_i^q. In lieu of a better indicator, the empirical analysis resorts to this proxy.

---

[11] An alternative line of argument in models of 'optimal speed of transition' and currency-crisis models of the second-generation type (see Sect. 2.3) stresses the level of unemployment instead of EU-aversion. However, I have given precedence to EU-aversion. The latter is more appropriate with respect to the developed interplay of powerful public approval and policy supply.

Table **6.4.** Levels of EU-aversion in CEECs

	2001	2002	2003	2003	2004	μ_i^q	σ_i^q
Czech Republic	0,09	0,14	0,13	0,15	0,17	0,14	0,02
Estonia	0,14	0,16	0,16	0,16	0,21	0,17	0,02
Hungary	0,07	0,05	0,07	0,10	0,15	0,09	0,03
Latvia	0,17	0,21	0,15	0,16	0,22	0,18	0,03
Lithuania	0,11	0,12	0,09	0,09	0,12	0,11	0,01
Poland	0,11	0,11	0,07	0,13	0,18	0,12	0,03
Slovakia	0,05	0,05	0,05	0,08	0,09	0,06	0,02
Slovenia	0,11	0,14	0,07	0,08	0,13	0,11	0,02

This section strived to approximate the probability q_i. At first, we argued in favour of changes in EU-aversion. For that purpose, we have run binomial logit regressions. In absence of reliable results, this part of the empirical examination refers to an alternative indicator. By utilizing an additional argument, this section maintains the level of EU-aversion establishing an appropriate proxy for estimating the probability q_i. The latter makes entrance into the stylized political forecast.

6.3 Computing the Probability for a Frugal EU

Another issue of the empirical analysis entails finding the probability of p, which denotes the likelihood of encountering a frugal EU-15, when a $CEEC_i$ opts for brinkmanship. The 'threaten-thy-neighbour'-strategy aims at eliciting financial transfers for CEECs. Such transfers are based on policies of 'Social and economic cohesion' within the EU. According structural policies are subject to legislative decision-making at the European level. Hence, we approximate the probability p by measuring the remaining influence of current EMU-members in political decision-making at the EU level, as soon as the CEECs have gained EU-membership status. This influence represents the EU-15's capability to block the prospective EMU-members demand for additional funding. Power indices measure to what extent influence is dependent on the voting mechanisms in place. Regarding the probability p, the estimation is based on the calculations of (normalized) Banzhaf-power indices. The selected estimate measures influence in relation to the voting-rules in the Council of Ministers. At the time of the CEECs' EU admittance in May 2004, the voting-rules agreed upon in the Treaty of Nice were valid – i.e. a 'simple' qualified majority vote (QMV) in the relevant field of 'Social and Economic Cohesion'. However, this voting-rule has since been replaced with a re-weighted QMV. This empirical analysis refers to the current re-weighted QMV.

The course for this part of the empirical examination is as follows: First, we briefly introduce the power-index concept, in particular the well-known Banzhaf index. Second, we provide the relevant voting-rule in the context of European structural policies. Finally, we calculate the probability p.

Generally speaking, the voting-power of a member in a decision-making body indicates the extent to which the member is able to affect the outcome of a ballot given a specified voting-rule. That is, power indices calculate ballot pivoting, which transform a portion of the voting-members into a winning coalition. Felsenthal and Machover [85] introduced the differentiation of two lines of power indices. On the one hand, there is the understanding of power as influence. The rationale of this concept is that the voting-outcome affects both the winning and the losing coalition. On the other hand, there is a concept of power putting emphasis on the prize to a winning coalition.[12] However, legislative decisions with reference to structural policies feature the usual characteristics of public goods and affect both current and prospective members either way. For this reason, the influence-power concept matches our discussion. In particular, the Banzhaf-power index produces the *a priori* probability for a pivotal voting-member. Gauging a voting-member's influence by its *a priori* probability is of particular relevance for our study. This is because it is *ex ante* contingent, which policy issues are subject to a bargain and are possibly linked [111]. Hence, the Banzhaf index is preference-free – i.e. the policy positions of voting-members are ignored (see, for further discussion, for instance, Sutter [196]). In this manner, this part of the empirical examination calculates the likelihood of a policy change induced by prospective members of the EMU. This corresponds, in turn, to the probability p of current members' ability to rebuff a CEEC's policy shifting actions. This applies, for instance, to issues of 'Social and economic cohesion' within the EU.[13]

The Banzhaf index just measures the relative influence of each voting-member. At the same time, it accounts for weighted votes, as well. A voting-member's influence power is calculated by recording

---

[12] In this respect, the Shapley-Shubik index is the most popular class of the prize-power indices.

[13] The line of argument coincides with the understanding of the 'strategic-power index' [195]. However, Felsenthal and Machover have proven that the authors' power index is a re-weighted Banzhaf-power index [86]. This supports even further the appropriateness of the Banzhaf index for this stylized political forecast.

swings. With such a swing, a crucial member enters a coalition, as a result of which a losing coalition is turned into a winning one. The absolute Banzhaf index is the sum of a voting-member's swings divided by the number of coalitions to which this specific pivot is attributed. In regard to our empirical examination, a desirable property of the power index is the sum of each voter's power adding up to one. The accordingly normalized Banzhaf index (nBI) is obtained by dividing the sum of a particular voting-member's swings by the sum of all voting-members' swings. The nBI is interpreted as a measurement of each voter's relative share among all pivotal positions.

Regarding the provision of financial transfers and funds, the precise decision-making rules are laid down in Title XVII ('Social and economic cohesion') of the Treaty establishing the European Community amended by the Treaty of Nice: Albeit, the rules for the provision of structural funds [European Agricultural Guidance and Guarantee Fund (EAGGF), European Social Fund (ESF), European Regional Development Fund (ERDF)] and the Cohesion Fund[14] as specified in the Article 161 (ex Article 130d) remain unchanged – i.e. an unanimously acting Council of Ministers. article has been considerably amended by the Treaty of Nice: "If specific actions prove necessary outside the funds" (Article 159 (ex Article 130b)) QMV, as well as the co-decision procedure (Article 251 (ex Article 189b)) are still in force.[15] After the admittance of ten new EU-members in May 2004, the Council of Ministers is now comprised of 25 voting-members, which affect the estimated probability p. More precisely, p denotes the ability of current EMU-members to maintain a frugal attitude towards additional funding for new members after their accession.

In the presently valid voting-rule of the Council of Ministers a winning majority requires fulfilling three criteria: number of votes, number of members, and number of population.

This is to say that a winning coalition must have at least 232 votes of the 321 Council votes. In addition, it must also represent at least 50% of the EU-members. Finally, the winning coalition must represent at least 62% of the EU population. This complicated triple criteria thresh-

---

[14] Regarding the Cohesion Fund, this is especially a 'Spanish success': It has been decided to switch to QMV, but this will not apply until after the adoption of the multi-annual financial perspectives applicable as of 2007.

[15] The co-decision procedure concerns the approval by the European Parliament (EP) in legislative decision-making. However, the subsequent calculations leave the influence of the EP aside.

Table 6.5. Influence power in an EU-25

	Votes	Pop. in 1000	nBI*100
France	29	59900,7	8,56
Germany	29	82531,7	8,56
Italy	29	57888,2	8,56
United Kingdom	29	59651,5	8,56
Poland	27	38190,6	8,12
Spain	27	42345,2	8,12
Netherlands	13	16258,0	4,23
Belgium	12	10396,0	3,91
Czech Republic	12	10211,5	3,91
Greece	12	11041,1	3,91
Hungary	12	10116,7	3,91
Portugal	12	10474,7	3,91
Austria	10	8114,0	3,27
Sweden	10	8975,7	3,27
Slovakia	7	5380,1	2,31
Denmark	7	5397,6	2,31
Estonia	7	1350,6	2,31
Finland	7	5219,7	2,31
Ireland	7	4027,5	2,31
Latvia	4	2319,2	1,33
Lithuania	4	3445,9	1,33
Slovenia	4	1996,4	1,33
Cyprus	4	730,4	1,33
Luxembourg	4	451,6	1,33
Malta	3	399,9	0,99
TOT	321	456814,6	100

old makes the calculations of power indices time-intensive. The results of the calculations for each EU-member's influence power are displayed in Table 6.5.[16] The probability p is the remaining influence power of the EU-15 (plus Cyprus and Malta) in an EU-25. This way, we simply subtract the power of the CEECs. Their power demonstrates the *a priori* probability of influencing an outcome in legislative decision-making processes at the European level. The remainder is the quasi influence power of the EU-15 – i.e. the likelihood of encountering a frugal EU-15 in the two-stage threat game. The relative share of influence for each

---

[16] The weighted votes are taken from [14], whereas the power indices have been calculated by using 'Indices of Power' - IOP 2.0 [32]. Data on population is taken from Eurostat http://epp.eurostat.cec.eu.int; January 26, 2005.

member of the EU-15 adds up to an estimated $p = 75\%$.

In the previous paragraphs we have set up input cost parameters, as well as the estimates for EU-aversion within the CEECs' constituencies and for encountering a frugal EU-15. In a next step, we process these data in a Monte-Carlo simulation. The stylized model brings forth probability forecasts for a CEEC to practise brinkmanship in ERM II.

6.4 Monte-Carlo Simulation of Threat Game Bounds

Monte-Carlo methods are a class of computational algorithms for simulating, for instance, the behaviour of political and economic systems. Such simulation makes allowances for data uncertainty in input parameters and variables in terms of using random sampling from particular probability distributions – i.e. we assume normal distribution of continuous random variables. In doing so, all inputs are reinterpreted in the form of a stochastic model. This way, it is possible to estimate probability forecasts on the basis of distribution functions or integrals of density functions with complicated boundary conditions. This mirrors the case in our threat game: Probability estimates rely on multidimensional integrals of density functions of various cost parameters. These integral boundaries are the effectiveness and acceptability condition which are non-linear functions of the costs involved. While every linear combination of normally distributed and continuous random variables is also normally distributed, this is not necessarily the case for non-linear functions of normally distributed continuous random variables. For this reason, we utilize a Monte-Carlo simulation.

In general, our approach resembles the work of Cioffi-Revilla [49] in political science.[17] This applies particularly to dealings with non-linear relations and related probability estimations. In our political-economic context, we presume normal probability distribution for all continuous random variables throughout the Monte-Carlo simulations. In order to make further allowances for data uncertainty we consider a baseline, optimistic, and pessimistic scenario analysis for the estimated cost parameters (C_i^C) and (C^D). This approach further highlights the non-linear relation underlying credible threatening and successful brinkmanship in ERM II.

---

[17] Monte-Carlo simulations are often used in finance and biometrics. Only recently have such methods entered areas of political science, particularly in its econometric strand [121]

This portion of the empirical analysis sketches the probability of each CEEC_i altering its exchange-rate policy stance in ERM II, i.e. practising brinkmanship. We have already dealt with the effectiveness and acceptability condition in detail. Both conditions constitute the upper and lower bounds (see (5.8) and (5.9)) for potentially successful brinkmanship. Stochastic cost parameters determine these bounds. As mentioned above, the credibility of threatening and thus, successful brinkmanship, depend on potential voter alienation within a CEEC_i in the course of adhering to Maastricht criteria in ERM II. This particular relation is depicted in terms of the probability $\mathcal{P}_{q_i}(q_i^* | q_{i,\min} < q_i^* < q_{i,\max})$. However, this condition for credible threatening also hinges on the probability $\mathcal{P}_p(p^* | p^* < p_{\max})$. The latter depicts the probability with which the voting-power value p^* of encountering a frugal EU-15 is smaller than $p_{\max}$, which, in turn, depends on the stochastic cost parameters. The idea is to calculate the conditional probability $\mathcal{P}_i(Q_i^* \cap P^*)$ – i.e. the appropriate conditional probability of $\mathcal{P}_{q_i}(q_i^* | q_{i,\min} < q_i^* < q_{i,\max})$ and $\mathcal{P}_p(p^* | p^* < p_{\max})$ – with which threatening is perceived as credible. This outcome then demonstrates the probability with which a CEEC will practise brinkmanship when passing through ERM II.

In the following paragraphs, we seek to estimate the probability $\mathcal{P}_i(Q_i^* \cap P^*)$. This process is broken down into several parts. Basically, we proceed along the lines of the (5.4)–(5.6). That is, we estimate the stochastic values of

$$q_{i,\min} = f_{\min}(\mathbf{C}) = \frac{c_i}{\sum_{i=1}^n \lambda_i + 1} \quad \text{with} \quad c_i = \frac{1}{2}\lambda_i \,,$$

$$q_{i,\max} = f_{\max}(\mathbf{C}) = c_i \frac{1-p}{p} \,, \quad \text{and}$$

$$p_{\max} = f_p(\mathbf{C}) = \frac{\sum_{i=1}^n \lambda_i + 1}{\sum_{i=1}^n \lambda_i + 2} < 1 \,,$$

while $\lambda_i = \frac{C^D}{C_i^C} - 1$ is the EU-15's limited liability according to proposition (5.1) and $\mathbf{C}$ is the column vector of $\mathbf{C}^T = (C^D, (\mathbf{C}^C)^T) = (C^D, C_1^C, ..., C_8^C)$ with $C^D \sim N(\mu^D, \sigma^D)$ and $C_i^C \sim N(\mu_i^C, \sigma_i^C)$. Firstly, we estimate $\mathcal{P}_{q_i}(q_i^* | q_{i,\min} < q_i^* < q_{i,\max})$. Secondly, we work out the density functions ϕ for probability estimations taking into account the covariance matrix of time-dependent output gap estimates – i.e. the costs of convergence – for the eight CEECs. Thirdly, we estimate the probability $\mathcal{P}_p(p^* | p^* < p_{\max})$ according to which the costs parameter driven $p_{\max}$ is greater than the expected value p^* of encountering a frugal EU-15. We then ultimately arrive at the conditional probability $\mathcal{P}_i(Q_i^* \cap P^*)$.

Density functions are required to estimate probabilities, which we compute with the help of Monte-Carlo simulations. In our analysis, nine stochastic cost parameters – i.e. one times the costs of default and eight times the costs of convergence for all CEECs – affect the computation of the ultimate conditional probability $\mathcal{P}_i$. The probability $\mathcal{P}_{q_i}(q_i^* | q_{i,\min} < q_i^* < q_{i,\max})$ is derived from

$$
\mathcal{P}_{q_i} = \int_{\{C | q_{i,\min} < q_i^* < q_{i,\max}\}} \phi_D(C^D)\phi_C(C_1^C, ..., C_8^C)dC^D dC_1^C, ..., dC_8^C
$$

$$
= \int_{\mathbb{R}^9} \chi_{q_i}\, \phi_D(C^D)\phi_C(C_1^C, ..., C_8^C)dC^D dC_1^C, ..., dC_8^C
$$

with the characteristic function

$$
\chi_{q_i} : X \mapsto \{0, 1\}, x \to
\begin{cases}
1 \text{ if } q_{i,\min} < \dfrac{\frac{1}{2}(\frac{C^D}{C_i^C} - 1)}{\sum_{i=1}^n \frac{C^D}{C_i^C}} < q_{i,\max} \\[4mm]
0 \text{ else}
\end{cases}
.
$$

This characteristic function χ_{q_i} is the mathematical expression for 'the level of EU-aversion is too small to be effective, thus, the EU-15 cannot be coerced into providing financial assistance' and 'the level of EU-aversion is too high to be acceptable for governments seeking survival'. This is, again, non-linearity in the relation of the effectiveness and acceptability condition. Regarding the density functions ϕ the density of costs of default has the familiar shape of

$$
\phi_D(C^D) = \frac{1}{\sigma^D \sqrt{2\pi}} e^{-\frac{1}{2}\frac{(\tilde{c}^D - \mu^D)^2}{(\sigma^D)^2}} .
$$

Whereas, the joint multidimensional density function of the costs of convergence is in vector notation

$$
\phi_C(\mathbf{C}^C) = \frac{1}{\sqrt{(2\pi)^8 det \mathbf{A}}} e^{-\frac{1}{2}(\mathbf{C}^C)^T \mathbf{A}^{-1} \mathbf{C}^C}
$$

with the covariance matrix $\mathbf{A}$ and the according inverse covariance matrix $\mathbf{A}^{-1}$ of the costs of convergence.

The covariance matrix $\mathbf{A}$ can be constructed with the help of a Pearson pairwise correlation matrix for the case of normally distributed C_i^C. For this purpose, we draw upon the output gap estimates (see Table 6.1) which are the residuals of the HP-trend components of CEECs real GDP growth rates and are distinguished into the three alternative scenarios. The Pearson correlation matrix tests time-dependency of those costs of convergence. Because of the normal distribution assumption we may simply extract covariances whenever there is significant correlation of output gap estimates. Such correlation indicates that an economic setback in one country has negative external effects on other countries' economic activity and vice versa. We find significant correlation among all Baltic countries and Slovakia, as well as a correlation between Hungary and Latvia.[18] The derived symmetric covariance matrix $\mathbf{A}$ has thus the form

$$
\mathbf{A} = \begin{pmatrix}
\sigma_{11}^C & & & & & & & \\
 & \sigma_{22}^C & & & & & & \\
 & & \sigma_{33}^C & & & & & \\
 & \sigma_{42}^C & \sigma_{44}^C & & & & & \\
 & \sigma_{52}^C & \sigma_{54}^C & \sigma_{55}^C & & & & \\
 & & & & \sigma_{66}^C & & & \\
 & \sigma_{72}^C & \sigma_{74}^C & \sigma_{75}^C & & \sigma_{77}^C & & \\
 & & & & & & \sigma_{88}^C
\end{pmatrix}.
$$

The diagonal shows the variances of costs of convergence. The lower off-diagonal displays only the significant covariances derived from the symmetric correlation matrix.

Now, we have the necessary figures to compute $\mathcal{P}_q$. The latter has to be re-weighted with the probability $\mathcal{P}_p(p^* \mid p^* < p_{max})$ in order to obtain the ultimate conditional probability $\mathcal{P}_i(Q_i^* \cap P^*)$. For the time being, we need to estimate the density function again with the help of a multidimensional integral

$$
\mathcal{P}_p = \int_{\{\mathbf{C}\mid p_{max} > p^*\}} \phi_D(C^D)\phi_C(C_1^C, ..., C_8^C)dC^D dC_1^C, ..., dC_8^C \ .
$$

At this stage, we have all the required information at our disposal to facilitate the Monte-Carlo simulations. These simulations are distinguished into a baseline, optimistic, and pessimistic scenario. We

---

[18] It can be conjectured that the use of the HP-filter really 'filters' a lot of correlation in the residual component. A possible reason is that the correlation is encapsulated in the trend components. Note that the correlation coefficients are not displayed.

generate a random sample of 75 observations with 10,000 iterations.[19] Skewness-kurtosis tests indicate that the normal distribution assumption for intermediate results can be maintained at conventional significance levels, i.e. 95%- and mostly 99%- significance. The resulting conditional probabilities for credible threats – i.e. CEECs to practise brinkmanship in ERM II – are displayed in Table 6.6 in the subsequent section.

6.5 Syncretism of Empirical Analysis

The preceding sections of the empirical analysis have inquired into the estimations for cost parameters and probabilities of the two-stage threat game. At this stage, all relevant information for a stylized political forecast are available. Based on the information, we first gather the CEECs that will likely practise brinkmanship in ERM II. Second, we sketch the size of financial transfers that the CEECs may elicit from the current EMU-members by making use of the 'threaten-thy-neighbour'-strategy. Accordingly, the stylized political forecast puts forth the costs that may arise in the course of the CEECs' passing through ERM II. Finally, the costs involved are compared with the financial budgeting of the EU. This way, we gain an appreciation for the potential financial burden attached to required systemic stabilization of CEECs' EMU admission.

Table 6.6 summarizes all substantial results.

It appears that the three Baltic countries Estonia, Latvia, and Lithuania, as well as Hungary are eligible brinkmanship candidates. This result is hardly surprising because these are the countries with negative μ_i^C, i.e. those CEECs that are incurred with costs of convergence. In almost every scenario the brinkmanship strategy for these countries complies with the effectiveness and acceptability condition.

In each of these cases, there is 'enough' – to put it simply – of the estimated q_i that falls into the interval of $q_{i,min}$ to $q_{i,max}$ as highlighted in the column of $\mathcal{P}_{q_i}$. Hence, these countries potentially present at least an effective threat. However, the scenario analysis indicates that 50% alterations to estimated costs of convergence may lead to lower probabilities of successful brinkmanship. This reflects the non-linearity that possesses the threaten-thy-neighbour strategy: Higher costs of convergence may buttress the effectiveness condition, but may

---

[19] This number of replications should be 'random enough'. Note that a change in the number of randomly generated observations invalidates the normal distribution of some simulation outcomes.

Table **6.6.** Empirical syncretism

Country	Scen.	$q_{i,min}$	q_i	$q_{i,max}$	P_{q_i}	P_p	P_i
	B	0,04 (0,17)	0,14 (0,02)	-0,26 (0,39)	0	0,99	0
Czech Republic	O	0,05 (0,16)	0,14 (0,02)	-0,30 (0,38)	0	0,43	0
	P	0,02 (0,17)	0,14 (0,02)	-0,21 (0,39)	0	0,32	0
	B	0,01 (0,14)	0,17 (0,02)	-0.03 (0,38)	0,13	0,99	0,13
Estonia	O	0,02 (0,13)	0,17 (0,02)	-0,10 (0,39)	0,07	0,43	0,03
	P	0 (0,15)	0,17 (0,02)	0,02 (0,38)	0,17	0,32	0,05
	B	0 (0,10)	0,09 (0,03)	-0,01 (0,38)	0,09	0,99	0,09
Hungary	O	0 (0,10)	0,09 (0,03)	-0.09 (0.39)	0,02	0,43	0,01
	P	0 (0,10)	0,09 (0,03)	0,05 (0,36)	0,15	0,32	0,05
	B	-0,01 (0,13)	0,18 (0,03)	0,10 (0,34)	0,27	0,99	0,27
Latvia	O	0 (0,12)	0,18 (0,03)	-0,01 (0,38)	0,19	0,43	0,08
	P	-0,01 (0,12)	0,18 (0,03)	0,15 (0,28)	0,33	0,32	0,11
	B	0 (0,10)	0,11 (0,01)	-0,09 (0,39)	0,12	0,99	0,12
Lithuania	O	0 (0,10)	0,11 (0,01)	-0,13 (0,39)	0,09	0,43	0,04
	P	0 (0,20)	0,11 (0,01)	-0,07 (0,39)	0	0,32	0
	B	0,04 (0,17)	0,12 (0,03)	-0,31 (0,38)	0	0,99	0
Poland	O	0,06 (0,17)	0,12 (0,03)	-0,38 (0,36)	0	0,43	0
	P	0,02 (0,18)	0,12 (0,03)	-0,25 (0,39)	0	0,32	0
	B	0 (0,20)	0,06 (0,02)	-0,22 (0,39)	0	0,99	0
Slovakia	O	0 (0,20)	0,06 (0,02)	-0,26 (0,39)	0	0,43	0
	P	0 (0,20)	0,06 (0,02)	-0,19 (0,40)	0	0,32	0
	B	0,04 (0,17)	0,11 (0,02)	-0,29 (0,39)	0	0,99	0
Slovenia	O	0,06 (0,17)	0,11 (0,02)	-0,34 (0,37)	0	0,43	0
	P	0,02 (0,17)	0,11 (0,02)	-0,22 (0,39)	0	0,32	0

also come at the expense of the acceptability condition and vice versa. This becomes especially apparent, for instance, in the case of Lithuania, which drops from the sample of eligible brinkmanship candidates in the pessimistic scenario. With regard to the acceptability condition, the estimated probability p is almost with certainty smaller than the conditional probability $p_{i,max}$ in the baseline scenario. These countries' brinkmanship also meets the acceptability condition in the alternative optimistic and pessimistic scenario – though, to a lesser extent.

Summarily, the probability for Estonia credibly threatening to practise brinkmanship in ERM II lies within a range of 3% in the optimistic and 13% in the baseline scenario. The according probabilities for Hungary are between 1% - 9% and for Latvia in the range of 8% - 27% with reference to all three scenarios. At the same time, there is a successful brinkmanship of Lithuania in the baseline (12%) and optimistic (4%) scenario. Yet, Lithuania foregoes the opportunity to burden the EU-15 with some costs of convergence in the pessimistic scenario. Generally speaking, these few examples point to the sensitivity of the equilibrium results: A small change in the parameters may invert both the effectiveness condition and the acceptability condition of the brinkmanship.

In reference to the game-theoretic analysis in Chap. 5 the overall result of this stylized political forecast for CEECs' behaviour in ERM II highlights that the strategy combination of (('ERM II', 'overvalue'), 'give in') constitutes the sub-game perfect Nash equilibrium of $\Gamma(\varsigma_i, d)$ for $i = \{2, 3, 4, 5\}$.

Moreover, we are also able to estimate the amount of costs involved in the two-stage threat game. Table 6.7 shows the shares of costs of convergence that CEECs pass onto current EMU-members.[20] According to the stylized political forecast, these costs range between 20–60 m. Euro for the Baltic countries, to 210 m. Euro for Hungary in 2005.

Table 6.7. Projected costs of convergence passed on to the EU-15

	GDP 2005(f)	$\hat{C}_i^C$ in % GDP	$\hat{C}_i^C$
Czech Republic	100,2	-	-
Estonia	9,9	-0,38	-0,04
Hungary	90,0	-0,47	-0,42
Latvia	11,7	-1,00	-0,12
Lithuania	19,8	-0,21	-0,04
Poland	233,3	-	-
Slovakia	37,1	-	-
Slovenia	27,9	-	-

Immediately after the eligible brinkmanship candidates' accession to ERM II and at the start of the 'threaten-thy-neighbour'-strategy, the EU-15 burdens itself, for instance, with up to 210 m. Euro with respect to Hungary's costs of convergence – i.e. the fifty-fifty split of $\hat{C}_5^C$. This is to say, that Hungary, in turn, is in a position to elicit about the same amount in terms of financial transfers from the EU-15.

---

[20] GDP data (in bn. Euro) are taken from Eurostat.

At this stage, the EU-15 keeps this particular $CEEC_i$ from continuing its 'threaten-thy-neighbour'-strategy.

If a $CEEC_i$'s brinkmanship results in a new institutional scheme for the distribution of structural funds – for instance, due to the principle of equal treatment within the EU, – then the EU-15 would be stuck with costs amounting to nc_i, i.e. here eight times a $CEEC_i$'s compensation payment in terms of % GDP. This is to say, that the EU-15 face additional costs amounting up to about 1.7 bn. Euro per annum. The sum is less than 0.2 per thousand of the EU-15's GDP (c. 10176 bn. Euro in 2005(f) according to Eurostat).

In comparison to the estimated additional fiscal costs amounting to 13–37.2 bn. Euro per annum (in 1999 prices) after the CEECs' admittance to the EU (see above), the forecasted costs of the CEECs' brinkmanship in ERM II are not excessive, but rather marginal. Additional fiscal costs, in terms of financial transfers to the CEECs, have a noticeable impact on the financial perspective of the EU-25. Nevertheless, potentially required fiscal transfers are a very small amount of costs for the EU-15 relative to its GDP. In the face of considerable economic and political costs of a stalled European integration process, completing the investment project 'EU-enlargement' is indeed a 'cheap deal' as suggested by Baldwin et al. [13]. Though, the provision of such additional funding and the systemic stabilization of the CEECs' adjustment process toward the eurozone may prove demanding for the EU-25. This subject appears in the concluding remarks.

7

Conclusions

This work has examined the political economy of exchange-rate policies in the context of the eastward enlargement of the eurozone. The peculiarities of this phase in the European integration process are at the heart of this thesis. This study has brought to the fore that the adjustments that CEECs may undergo for their EMU-membership may not turn out as anticipated but it is fraught with tensions. The prospective members of the EMU are likely to pass on some of the incurred Maastricht costs of convergence to the current EMU-members. The transmission mechanism is an altered exchange-rate policy that is carried out utilizing a 'threaten-thy-neighbour'-strategy. Such brinkmanship strategy consequently enables CEECs to wrest financial concessions from current members of the EMU. The nature of the arising conflict between current and prospective EMU-members originates form both parties' admitted inclination to complete the enlargement process, complicated by their disinclination to bear the costs.

The course of analysis has been as follows: Chap. 2 has set up a political-economic framework for the analysis of exchange-rate policy in the context of European integration. System-theoretic considerations have underpinned this analytical framework, and highlighted the supposed isomorphism of political and economic systems. In line with these considerations the study models exchange-rate policy as a public good stemming from the interplay of voter demand and politicians' policy supply. In addition, this portion of the study has the advantage of improving the accuracy of future analyses. In this way, the foundation has been laid out for the understanding of policy formation in the course of the enlargement process.

Chap. 3 has prepared the ground for the subsequent analysis of the CEECs' exchange-rate policy in ERM II. The analysis began with the critical assumption that the enlargement decision was a political decision aiming to stabilize CEE. The starting point is that the 'EU-enlargement' project is an investment in the joint provision of the public good 'political stability' in CEE. Consequently, this part of the analysis has arrived at the conclusion that the EU-15 has a willingness to pay for the CEECs' admittance. The argument is that the entire eastward enlargement process, which is completed with the introduction of the euro as legal tender in CEECs, can be regarded as a strictly competitive zero-sum game. In this respect, any intergovernmental agreement between current and prospective EMU-members constitutes a Nash-equilibrium in mixed strategies. In addition, the particular mixture of both parties' interests provokes free-riding behaviour. The ensuing moral-hazard behaviour of the CEECs proves to be one of brinkmanship.

The analysis in Chap. 4 is the heart of this study. This part of the thesis has elaborated on the details of the transmission mechanism of CEECs' brinkmanship. The latter consists of a hazardous stance towards exchange-rate policy, which has been denoted as a 'threaten-thy-neighbour'-strategy. The prescribed soft pegs in ERM II even encourage these countries in their resolve to practise brinkmanship. Moreover, the stability of the new member countries' exchange-rate regimes may be particularly at stake when adversities are taken into account, such as trend real appreciation and volatile capital flows. Eventually, a slackening of the reins of economic policy-making – most notably, fiscal policy – may put the exchange-rate regimes of CEECs in ERM II at risk, thus, triggering a currency crisis. It is important to note that a CEEC's successful brinkmanship will on no account entail a currency crisis – in that case such strategy would have failed. In the meantime, the according European governance structures fall short of effective precautions. The political-economic analysis of incentives of fixed exchange-rate regimes demonstrates that the prescribed soft pegs in ERM II make such 'threaten-thy-neighbour'-strategy even more palatable to CEECs.

The hallmark of this study is the game-theoretic modelling of the CEECs' exchange-rate policy formation in ERM II. The latter resembles a two-stage threat game – again, a strictly competitive zero-sum game, – which is unfolded in Chap. 5. The 'threaten-thy-neighbour'-strategy constitutes a deterrent threat dependent on the expounded effectiveness and acceptability condition. Deterrence rests on credibly threatening to trigger an exchange-rate crisis, thus spoiling the 'EU-enlargement' project and, consequently, the European integration process. The subsequent bargaining game results in a robust unique bargaining outcome. This sub-game perfect Nash equilibrium consists of an agreement upon sharing the costs of convergence in ERM II on a fifty-fifty basis.

The game-theoretic model is a skeleton. However, the stylized political forecast in Chap. 6 indicates that the theoretically derived hypotheses are empirically testable. In addition, the empirical account of a comprehensive Monte-Carlo simulation has contributed to an appreciation of the financial and political dimensions of the fierce bargain in ERM II. According to the simulation study, eligible brinkmanship candidates are the Baltic countries and Hungary, although dependant on the assumed baseline, optimistic, and pessimistic scenario. The hard bout of haggling over redistributing the Maastricht costs of convergence may result in a new institutional scheme of cohesion funds for CEECs amounting at most to about 1.7 bn. Euro per annum. Such a financial transfer is rather small when compared to the overall financial budget of the EU. This likely bargaining outcome is characterized and evaluated in the following paragraph.

Originally, the CEECs were to incur all the Maastricht costs of convergence in the course of qualifying for EMU-membership. These countries can try to redistribute these costs by deploying the 'threaten-thy-neighbour'-strategy. Accordingly, there are considerable distributive gains for CEECs in this bargaining. In regard to efficiency gains, each single bargaining outcome is a Pareto-efficient solution. However, this does not apply to the setting-up of a standard cohesion fund because in most instances the EU-15's expenses are higher than their actual willingness to pay for the public good 'political stability' in the case of bilateral negotiations. Nevertheless, both current and prospective members of the EMU gain from the completion of the 'EU-enlargement' project in terms of ensuring 'political Stability' in CEE.

Moreover, the system-theoretic considerations have outlined the benchmark for systemic stabilization. That is, it emphasizes the efficacy of policy in terms of achieving a particular goal, which is here the realization of the eastward enlargement of the eurozone. More precisely, intergovernmental policy solutions to negative external effects of national exchange-rate policy formation are assessed in terms of allowing for an effective internalization. The systemic stabilization of this enlargement process requires the amount of the aforementioned 1.7 bn. Euro per annum. The game-theoretic analysis has shown that there is then no further leeway for CEECs to elicit more than this amount, but such transfer is sufficient enough to stabilize this phase of the European integration process.

Whether or not the then enlarged EU and EMU are resilient systems, which facilitate smooth functioning for future decision-making processes, has not been a research topic addressed in this study. By the same token, we cannot make any assessments regarding the set up of new funds. This applies either way in terms of reshuffling within the EU-budget and by raising new financial contributions among EU-member countries. These questions are dedicated to future research. This study only makes judgements with regard to the eastward enlargement of the eurozone until the first day of introducing the euro as legal tender in CEECs. The systemic stabilization of this process affords a relatively small financial contribution.

A generalization of the research results of this study is easily extractable: The focus has been on the political economy of exchange-rate policy, though in the context of the eastward enlargement of the eurozone. However, when there is an applicant seeking membership in the EU-club – at whose admittance the 'ins' are also interested in, – then moral-hazard behaviour ensues. This applies to future EU-enlargement rounds, as well. Every 'member with a derogation' may be able to convert the moral hazard behaviour into brinkmanship within ERM II. The key is to engender a corresponding precarious exchange-rate policy. Such course of exchange-rate policy making is open to every applicant whose entrance is in the strong interest of the EU. Furthermore, it is also clear that the EMU-founders, when agreeing upon the Maastricht criteria structure, did not envisaged that the exchange-rate criterion prepares the ground for a 'threaten-thy-neighbour'-strategy. Obviously, some things never turn out the way you think they will.

In reference to policy advice, convenient recommendations are difficult to imagine. The study has already indicated that there are almost no effective countermeasures and precautions against CEEC's brinkmanship – to say the least. An effective economic policy coordination particularly in terms of fiscal surveillance is desirable. However, such surveillance is already in place and its efficacy fails due to the difficulty of keeping fiscal policies of sovereign countries in check. A potentially helpful measure would be to ask EU-members to relinquishing their fiscal sovereignty. Fiscal centralization may need to be undertaken in order to strengthen budgetary consolidation in the CEECs. This would eventually entail gathering fiscal competencies under the purview of a supranational European institution. However, it is rather unlikely that prospective, as well as current members are willing to let their most important economic-policy instrument get out of hand. As current members of the EMU are not disposed with a direct means to prevent CEECs from exercising brinkmanship when they have joined ERM II, the exclusion of soft pegs in ERM II might offer a possible remedy. Only floats would have to be allowed and ERM II fundamentally revised. However, betting on a revision of the Treaty establishing the European Community is a vain hope. Another drastic measure would be to enforce a quick introduction of the euro as legal tender in CEECs. In contrast to the ECB's present attitude towards early introduction of the euro, CEECs could be encouraged to euroize unilaterally. In doing so, current members of the EMU would forestall the CEECs from exhausting the EU-15's willingness to pay for 'political stability'. However, an early introduction of the euro may be detrimental to its price stability. This option confronts current members with a worst or a next-worst outcome. Therefore, the EU-15 is exposed to a 'Catch-22'-situation – i.e. caught between a rock and a hard place. The only feasible option left to keep the CEECs in check is to pay them for conducting prudent exchange-rate policies. Generally, two solutions are conceivable. Current members of the EMU may agree on (slightly) overvalued central parities in ERM II. Thereby giving the CEECs more access to resources, leading up to a welfare transfer from west to east. Or, as the study has primarily argued, both current and new members negotiate financial compensations alike, such as additional funds for CEECs. The latter outcome will easily enable them to ease the detrimental social and economic effects of their run-up to the EMU. This ensures the systemic stabilization of the CEECs' convergence toward the EMU, and a successful completion of the 'EU-enlargement' project.

At present, there are very few belated precautions foreseen. With regard to future enlargement rounds, a suitable measure would be to admit new applicants one after the other to the EU and the EMU. In this way, potential negative external effects of exchange-rate policy formation are stretched out over time. In such an instance, the 'ins' would avoid the sword of Damocles – i.e. possibly preventing the spread of defaults within a group of new EU-member countries. This would make the formation of deterrent threats more difficult, thus, sparing the EU-budget. Accordingly, things may work out well in the end – although, things may take a different course than originally imagined.

List of Figures

List of Tables

List of Symbols

H	superordinate bargaining game
M	set of players
$\mathbb{R}$	set of real numbers
j	subscript index for player 1 (CEEC$_i$) and 2 (EU-15)
i	subscript index for a multiple player 1 (CEEC$_i$)
S	set of strategies in H
u and v	players' utility functions
a, b, c	outcomes within the superordinate bargaining game H
G	bargaining game
s	set of strategies in G
$\mathbb{C}$	cartesian space of costs
B	benefits of integration (public good)
C^C	costs of convergence
C^D	costs of default
d	disagreement point
α and β	bargaining power coefficients
λ_i	limited liability of the EU-15
p and q	probability values
P and Q	finite probability sets
Γ	transformed bargaining game
c_i	specific bargaining outcome
R_{ij}	players' reaction functions
ι	utopian ideal point
τ	interval between alternating bargaining offers
t	time operator
δ	time-preferences
k and l	specific bargaining offers

$\mathbf{a}$ and $\mathbf{b}$	vector of equilibrium bargaining offers
ϱ	players' instantaneous rate of interest
μ	expectation value
σ	standard deviation
N	normal distribution
$\mathcal{P}$	joint probability set
χ	characteristic function
ϕ	density functions
$\mathbf{C}$	cost vector
$\tilde{c}^{\mathrm{D}}$	random number of cost of default
$\mathbf{A}$	covariance matrix
$\hat{C}_{\mathrm{i}}^{\mathrm{C}}$	projected costs of convergence

References

1. P. AGHION AND O. J. BLANCHARD (1994), *On the speed of transition in Central Europe*, NBER Working Paper, No. 4736.
2. A. ALESINA AND A. WAGNER (2003), *Choosing (and reneging on) exchange rate regimes*, NBER Working Paper, No. 9809.
3. F. ALLEN AND D. GALE (2000), *Financial contagion*, Journal of Political Economy, 108, pp. 1–33.
4. D. M. ANDREWS AND T. D. WILLETT (1997), *Financial interdependence and the state: International monetary relations at century's end*, International Organization, 51, pp. 479–511.
5. K. J. ARROW (1963), *Social choice and individual values*, Wiley, New York, NY, 2 ed.
6. ———(1984), *Utilities, attitudes, choices: A review note*, in: Individual Choice under Certainty and Uncertainty - Collected Papers of Kenneth J. Arrow, K. J. Arrow, ed., vol. 3, Basil Blackwell, Oxford, pp. 55–84.
7. M. ASPINWALL AND G. SCHNEIDER (2000), *Same menu, seperate tables: the institutionalist turn in political science and the study of European integration*, European Journal of Political Research, 38, pp. 1–36.
8. M. D. ASPINWALL (2000), *Creating stability: National preferences and the origins of European monetary system*, Center for European Studies - Working Paper Series, No. 9.
9. J. BABETSKI, L. BOONE, AND M. MAUREL (2003), *Exchange rate regimes and supply shocks asymmetry: the case of the accession countries*, CERGE-EI Working Paper, No. 206.
10. P. BACCHETTA (1994), *Spain and the real exchange rate problem*, in The monetary economics of Europe: causes of the EMS crisis, C. Johnson and S. Collignon, eds., Fairleigh Dickinson University Press, Rutherford, NJ, pp. 18–32.
11. B. BALASSA (1964), *The purchasing power parity doctrine: a reappraisal*, Journal of Political Economy, 72, pp. 584–596.
12. R. E. BALDWIN, E. BERGLÖF, F. GIAVAZZI, AND M. WIDGRÉN (2000), *EU reforms for tomorrow's Europe*, CEPR Discussion Paper, No. 2623.

13. R. E. BALDWIN, J. F. FRANCOIS, AND R. PORTES (1997), *The costs and benefits of Eastern enlargement: the impact on the EU and Eentral Europe*, Economic Policy, 12, pp. 125–176.

14. R. E. BALDWIN AND M. WIDGRÉN (2003), *Decision-making and the constitutional treaty: will the IGC discard Giscard?*, CEPS Policy Brief, No. 37.

15. S. BALIGA AND R. SERRANO (1995), *Multilateral bargaining with imperfect information*, Journal of Economic Theory, 67, pp. 578–589.

16. J. S. BANKS AND J. DUGGAN (2000), *A bargaining model of collective choice*, American Political Science Review, 94, pp. 73–88.

17. R. J. BARRO AND D. GORDON (1983), *Rules, discretion and reputation in a model of monetary policy*, Journal of Monetary Economics, 12, pp. 101–122.

18. R. J. BARRO AND X. SALA-I MARTIN (1995), *Technological diffusion, convergence, and growth*, NBER Working Paper, No. 5151.

19. G. S. BECKER (1983), *A theory of competition among pressure groups for political influence*, Quarterly Journal of Economics, 98, pp. 371–400.

20. D. BEGG (1998), *Pegging out: lessons from the Czech exchange rate crisis*, CEPR Discussion Paper, No. 1956.

21. D. BEGG, B. EICHENGREEN, L. HALPERN, J. V. HAGEN, AND C. WYPLOSZ (2003), *Sustainable regimes of capital movements in accession countries*, CEPR Policy Paper, No. 10.

22. K. BINMORE (1987), *The economics of bargaining*, Oxford University Press, Oxford.

23. ———(1992), *Fun and games: a text on game theory*, Heath, Lexington, MA.

24. S. BIRCH (2001), *Electoral systems and party system stability in post-communist europe*, mimeo.

25. N. BJÖRKSTÉN (2000), *Real convergence in the enlarged Euro area: a coming challenge for monetary policy*, Bank of Finland - Economics Department Working Paper, No.1.

26. T. E. A. BOERI (2002), *Who's afraid of the big enlargement? Economic and social implications of the European Union's prospective Eastern expansion*, CEPR Policy Paper, No. 7.

27. P. BOFINGER (1999), *Options for the exchange rate policies of the EU accession countries (and other emerging market economies)*, mimeo.

28. P. BOFINGER AND T. WOLLMERSHÄUSER (2002), *Exchange rate policies for the transition to EMU*, in: Alternative Monetary Regimes in Entry to EMU, U. Sepp and M. Randveer, eds., Bank of Estonia, Tallinn, pp. 95–132.

29. M. BOLLE (1975), *Wirtschaftskybernetik und Makroplanung: Systemtheoretische Analyse ökonomischer Makromodelle*, in: Systemtheorie und sozio-ökonomische Anwendungen, J. Baetge, ed., Dunker & Humblot, Berlin, pp. 1–35.

30. M. D. BORDO (1998), *International rescues versus bailouts: a historical perspective.*, mimeo.

31. M. D. BORDO, B. EICHENGREEN, D. KLINGEBIEL, AND M. S. MARTINEZ-PERIA (2001), *Is the crisis problem growing more severe?*, Economic Policy, 16, pp. 52–82.

32. T. BRÄUNINGER AND T. KÖNIG (2001), *Indices of power - IOP 2.0*, Konstanz: University of Konstanz.

33. H. BRÜCKER, P. J. SCHRÖDER, AND C. WEISE (2004), *Doorkeepers and gatecrashers: EU enlargement and negotiation strategies*, Journal of European Integration, 26, pp. 3–24.

34. J. M. BUCHANAN (1975), *The limits of liberty: between anarchy and the Leviathan*, University of Chicago Press, Chicago, IL.

35. ——(1989), *Essays on the political economy*, University of Hawaii Press, Honolulu, HI.

36. J. M. BUCHANAN AND G. TULLOCK (1962), *The calculus of consent: logical foundations of constitutional democracy*, University of Michigan Press, Ann Arbor, MI.

37. J. M. BUCHANAN AND Y. J. YOON (2003), *A correction in elementary public choice geometry*, Public Choice, 115, pp. 285–298.

38. W. H. BUITER AND C. GRAFE (2002), *Anchor, float or abandon ship: Exchange rate regimes for the accession countries*, CEPR Discussion Paper, No. 3184.

39. S. BULMER AND C. LEQUESNE (2002), *New perspectives on EU-member state relationships*, Questions de recherche / Research in Questions, No. 4.

40. DEUTSCHE BUNDESBANK (2001), *Währungspolitische Aspekte der EU-Erweiterung*, Monatsberichte der Deutschen Bundesbank (Oktober), pp. 15–31.

41. M. BURKART AND K. WALLNER (2000), *Club enlargement: early versus late admittance*, CEPR Discussion Paper, No. 2600.

42. H.-P. BURTH (1996), *Zur Verbindung von autopioetischer Systemtheorie und strukturell-individualistischer Handlungstheorie - vom system-theoretischen Makro-Imperialismus zur Mikro-Makro-Integration*, in: Handlungs- und Entscheidungstheorie in der Politikwissenschaft: Eine Einführung in Konzepte und Forschungsgegenstand, U. Druwe and V. Kunz, eds., Leske + Budrich, Opladen, pp. 226–241.

43. M. BUSSIÈRE AND C. MULDER (2000), *Political instability and economic vulnerability*, International Journal of Finance and Economics, 5, pp. 309–330.

44. L. CALMFORS (1998), *Macroeconomic policy, wage setting, and employment - what difference does the EMU make?*, Oxford Review of Economic Policy, 14, pp. 125–151.

45. A. CARLING (1995), *The paradox of voting and the theory of social evolution*, in: Preferences, Institutions and Rational Choice, K. Dowding and D. King, eds., Oxford University Press, Oxford, pp. 20–42.

46. A. B. ÇAMBEL (1989), *An overview of self-organization in social structures*, in: Dissipative Strukturen in Integrierten Systemen, A. B. Çambel, B. Fritsch, and J. U. Keller, eds., vol. 2 of Schriftenreihe zur gesellschaftlichen Entwicklung, Nomos, Baden-Baden, pp. 111–131.

47. CCEB (2003), *Candidate countries Eurobarometer 2003.2: public opinion in the candidate countries*.

48. CEEB (1997), *Central and Eastern Eurobarometer 8*.

49. C. CIOFFI-REVILLA (1998), *Politics and uncertainty: theory, models and applications*, Cambridge University Press, Cambridge, MA.

50. R. H. COASE (1960), *The problem of social cost*, Journal of Law and Economics, 3, pp. 1–44.

51. J. S. COLEMAN (1990), *Foundations of social theory*, Harvard University Press, Cambridge, MA.

52. F. CORICELLI (2002), *Exchange rate policy during transition to the European Monetary Union: The option of euroization*, Economics of Transition, 10, pp. 405–417.

53. F. CORICELLI AND B. JAZBEC (2001), *Real exchange rate dynamics in transition economies*, CEPR Discussion Paper, No. 2869.

54. R. CORKER, C. BEAUMONT, R. VAN ELKAN, AND D. IAKOVA (2000), *Exchange rate regimes in selected advanced transition economies - coping with transition, capital inflows, and EU accession*, IMF Policy Discussion Paper, No. 3.

55. V. P. CRAWFORD (1982), *A theory of disagreement in bargaining*, Econometrica, 50, pp. 607–637.

56. A. D. CROMBRUGGHE (2001), *Policy options for joining the Euro*, mimeo.

57. M. DE BROECK AND T. SLØK (2001), *Interpreting real exchange rate movements in transition countries*, BOFIT Discussion Papers, No. 7.

58. P. DE GRAUWE (1997), *Problems of transition and initialization of EMU*, Swedish Economic Policy Review, 4, pp. 117–154.

59. A. T. DENZAU AND R. PARKS (1977), *A problem with public sector preferences*, Journal of Economic Theory, 14, pp. 454–457.

60. A. T. DENZAU AND R. P. PARKS (1979), *Deriving public sector preferences*, Journal of Public Economics, 11, pp. 335–352.

61. K. W. DEUTSCH (1963), *The nerves of government: models of political communication and control*, Free Press of Glencoe, New York, NY.

62. B. DIBA AND A. M. FELDMAN (1984), *Utility functions of public outputs and majority voting*, Journal of Public Economics, 25, pp. 235–243.

63. H. DICKE AND F. FODERS (2000), *Wirtschaftliche Auswirkungen einer EU-Erweiterung auf die Mitgliedstaaten*, Mohr Siebeck, Tübingen.

64. D. G. DICKINSON AND J.-B. DESQUILBET (2001), *Joining EMU as an irreversible investment*, in: Financial and monetary integration in the new Europe: convergence between the EU and Central and Eastern Europe, D. G. Dickinson and A. W. Mullineux, eds., Edward Elgar, Cheltenham, pp. 224–251.

65. A. DIXIT AND S. SKEATH (1999), *Games of strategy*, W.W. Norton, New York, London.

66. A. DOWNS (1957), *An economic theory of democracy*, Harper and Row, New York, NY.

67. A. DRAZEN (2000), *Political economy of macroeconomics*, Princeton University Press, Princeton, NJ.

68. U. DRUWE (1989), *Rekonstruktion der "Theorie der Autopoiese" als Gesellschafts- und Steuerungsmodell*, in: Politische Steuerung sozialer Systeme, A. Görlitz, ed., Centaurus, Pfaffenweiler, pp. 35–58.

69. W. F. DUISENBERG (2001), *The ECB and the accession process*, mimeo.

70. ECB (1999), *Inflation differentials in a monetary union*, ECB Monthly Bulletin (October), pp. 36–45.

71. ——(2002), *The Eurosystem's dialogue with EU accession countries*, ECB Monthly Bulletin (July), pp. 51–63.

72. B. EICHENGREEN AND M. D. BORDO (2002), *Crises now and then: what lessons from the last era of financial globalization?*, NBER Working Paper, No. 8716.

73. B. EICHENGREEN AND R. HAUSMANN (1999), *Exchange rates and financial fragility*, NBER Working Paper, No. 7418.

74. B. EICHENGREEN AND P. MASSON (1998), *Exit strategies: policy options for countries seeking greater exchange rate flexibility*, IMF Occasional Paper, No. 168.

75. B. EICHENGREEN, A. K. ROSE, AND C. WYPLOSZ (1995), *Exchange rate mayhem: the antecedents and aftermath of speculative attacks*, Economic Policy, 21, pp. 249–312.

76. ——(1996), *Contagious currency crises*, NBER Working Paper, No. 5681.

77. R. V. ELKAN, R. A. FELDMAN, L. KUIJS, AND C. M. WATSON (2002), *Monetary and exchange rate regimes*, in: Into the EU: Policy Frameworks in Central Europe, R. A. Feldman and C. M. Watson, eds., IMF, Washington, DC.

78. M. ELLER AND P. HAISS (2002), *Integrationstheoretische, aussenhandelsseitige und finanzsektorspezifische Analyse der Teilnahme der mittel- und osteuropäischen Länder am EURO-Währungsraum*, Osteuropa-Wirtschaft, 47, pp. 200–215.

79. G. ERDMANN AND B. FRITSCH (1989), *Sysnergismen in sozialen Systemen, ein Anwendungsbeispiel*, in: Dissipative Strukturen in Integrierten Systemen, A. B. Çambel, B. Fritsch, and J. U. Keller, eds., Nomos, Baden-Baden, pp. 239–261.

80. EU (1997), *Resolution of the European council on the establishment of an exchange-rate mechanism in the third stage of Economic and Monetary Union, Amsterdam, 16 june 1997*, Official Journal C 236 , 02/08/1997 P. 0005 - 0006 31997Y0802(03).

81. EU-COMMISSION (2003), *2003 pre-accession economic programmes of acceding and other candidate countries: overview and assessment*, Enlargement Papers, No. 20.

82. J. D. FEARON (1994), *Signalling versus the balance of power and interests: An empirical test of a crisis bargaining model*, Journal of Conflict Resolution, 38, pp. 236–296.

83. ——(1997), *Signaling foreign policy interests: tying hands versus sinking costs*, Journal of Conflict Resolution, 41, pp. 68–90.

84. ——(1998), *Bargaining, enforcement, and international cooperation*, International Organization, 52, pp. 269–305.

85. D. S. FELSENTHAL AND M. MACHOVER (1998), *The measurement of voting power: theory and practice, problems and paradoxes*, Edward Elgar, Cheltenham, UK.

86. ——(2001), *Myths and meanings of voting power: comments on a symposium*, Journal of Theoretical Politics, 13, pp. 81–97.

87. J. FIDRMUC (2002), *Strategic aspects of exchange rate regime choice for the accession countries*, mimeo.

88. R. K. FILER AND J. HANOUSEK (2000), *Output changes and inflationary bias in transition*, CERGE-EI Working Paper, No. 167.

89. R. P. FLOOD AND N. MARION (1999), *Perspectives on the recent currency crisis literature*, NBER Working Paper, No. 6380.

90. A. FÖLSZ (2003), *The monetary framework after accession - a political economy analysis of ERM2*, European Integration online Papers (EIoP), 7, pp. 1–19.

91. P. W. V. FOREEST AND C. G. DE VRIES (2002), *The forex regime and EMU expansion*, Tinbergen Institute Discussion Paper, No. 10/2.

92. J. A. FRANKEL AND A. K. ROSE (1996), *The endogenity of the optimum currency area criteria*, NBER Working Paper, No. 5700.

93. M. FRATIANNI AND J. V. HAGEN (1992), *The European Monetary System and European Monetary Union*, Westview Press, Boulder, Oxford.

94. J. A. FRENKEL AND M. L. MUSSA (1980), *The efficiency of foreign exchange markets and measures of turbulence*, American Economic Review, 70, pp. 374–381.

95. ——(1985), *Asset markets, exchange rates, and the balance of payments*, in: Handbook of International Economics, R. W. Jones and P. B. Kenen, eds., North-Holland, Amsterdam, pp. 679–747.

96. G. FRIEBEL, L. NILSSON, AND K. WALLNER (1999), *Enlargement of the EU: What are prospects for success*, mimeo.

97. J. FRIEDEN AND L. L. MARTIN (2002), *International political economy: global and domestic interactions*, in: Political Science: State of the Discipline, I. Katznelson and H. V. Milner, eds., W.W. Norton, New York, London, pp. 118–146.

98. J. A. FRIEDEN (2002), *Real sources of European currency policy: Sectoral interests and European monetary integration*, International Organization, 56, pp. 831–860.

99. P. GÁSPÁR (2001), *Real and nominal convergence of pre-accession economies and the choice of exchange rate regime*, mimeo.

100. F. GIAVAZZI AND A. GIOVANNINI (1991), *Limiting exchange rate flexibility*, MIT Press, Cambridge, MA, 3 ed.

101. S. GOMULKA (2003), *Policy challenges within the (enlarged) European Union: how can economic convergence be fostered?*, in: Economic Convergence and Divergence in Europe: Growth and Regional Development in an Enlarged European Union, G. Tumpel-Gugerell and P. Mooslechner, eds., Edward Elgar, Cheltenham, pp. 436–447.

102. R. GRAFSTEIN (1991), *Rational choice: theory and institutions*, in: The Economic Approach to Politics: A Critical Reassesment of the Theory of Rational Action, K. R. Monereo, ed., Harper Collins, New York, NY, pp. 259–278.

103. E. GRANDE (2000) *Multi-Level Governance: Institutionelle Besonderheiten und Funktionsbedingungen des europäischen Mehrebenensystems*, in: Wie problemlösungsfähig ist die EU? Regieren im europäischen Mehrebenensystem, E. Grande and M. Jachtenfuchs, eds., Nomos, Baden-Baden, pp. 11–30.

104. D. GROS (2002), *The Euro at 25 - Special report of the CEPS Macroeconomic Policy Group*, Centre for European Policy Studies, Brussels.

105. J. V. HAGEN AND J. ZHOU (2002), *The choice of exchange rate regimes: an empirical analysis for transition economies*, ZEI Working Paper, B 03.

106. P. A. HALL AND R. C. TAYLOR (1996), *Political science and the three new institutionalisms*, MPIfG Discussion Paper, No. 96/6.

107. M. HALLERBERG AND L. VINHAS DE SOUZA (2000), *The political business cycles of EU accession countries.*, Tinbergen Institute Discussion Papers, No. 85/2.

108. J. C. HARSANYI AND R. SELTEN (1988), *A general theory of equilibrium selection in games*, MIT Press, Cambridge, MA.

109. F. A. HAYEK (1976), *Economics and knowledge*, in: Individualism and Economic Order, F. A. Hayek, ed., Routledge and Kegan Paul, London and Henley, pp. 33–56.

110. M. J. HOLLER AND G. ILLING (2003), *Einführung in die Spieltheorie*, Springer, Berlin, Heidelberg, New York, 5 ed.

111. M. J. HOLLER AND M. WIDGRÉN (1999), *Why power indices for assessing European Union decision-making?*, Journal of Theoretical Politics, 11, pp. 321–330.

112. C. S. HOLLING (1973), *Resilience and stability of ecological systems*, Annual Review of Ecology and Systematics, 4, pp. 1–23.

113. J. HÖLSCHER (2002), *Over- or undervalued euroland entry?*, mimeo.

114. B. R. HORNUNG (1988), *Grundlagen einer problemfunktionalistischen Systemtheorie gesellschaftlicher Entwicklung: sozialwissenschaftliche Theoriekonstruktion mit qualitativen, computergestützten Verfahren*, Lang, Frankfurt a.M.

115. F. IACONE AND R. ORSI (2002), *Exchange rate management and infla-tion targeting in the CEE accession countries*, Ezoneplus Working Paper, No. 8.

116. IMF (2000), *World Economic Outlook 2000*, vol. 2 (October), Interna-tional Monetary Fund, Washington, DC.

117. ——(2001), *World Economic Outlook 2001*, vol. 2 (October), Interna-tional Monetary Fund, Washington, DC.

118. ——(2004), *World Economic Outlook 2004*, vol. 2 (September), Inter-national Monetary Fund, Washington, DC.

119. R. INGLEHART (1971), *Changing value priorities and European integra-tion*, Journal of Common Market Studies, 10, pp. 1–36.

120. A. INOTAI (2000), *Political, economic and social arguments in favour of and against enlargement of the European Union: a review of influential pressure groups*, European Urban and Regional Studies, 7, pp. 269–280.

121. S. JACKMAN (2000), *Estimation and inference via Bayesian simulation: an introduction to Markov Chain Monte Carlo*, American Journal of Political Science, 44, pp. 369–398.

122. E. KALAI AND M. SMORODINSKY (1975), *Other solutions to Nash's bargaining problem*, Econometrica, 43, pp. 513–518.

123. G. L. KAMINSKI AND C. M. REINHART (1998), *The twin crises: the causes of banking of balance-of-payments problems*, mimeo.

124. O. KECK (1997), *Zur sozialen Konstruktion des Rational-Choice-Ansatzes - Einige Klarstellungen zur Rationalismus-Konstruktivismus-Debatte*, Zeitschrift für Internationale Beziehungen, 4, pp. 139–151.

125. P. KEEFER AND D. STASAVAGE (2001), *Checks and balances, private information, and the credibility of monetary commitments*, World Bank Working Papers Governance, Corruption, Legal Reform, No. 2542.

126. R. A. KEOHANE (1984), *After hegemony: cooperation and discord in the world political economy*, Princeton University Press, Princeton, NJ.

127. ——(1982), *The demand for international regimes*, International Orga-nization, 36, pp. 325–355.

128. H.-D. KLINGEMANN AND B. WESSELS (2002), *Sincere voting in differ-ent electoral systems*, mimeo.

129. V. KLYUEV (2001), *A model of exchange rate regime choice in the tran-sitional economies of Central and Eastern Europe*, IMF Working Paper, No. 140.

130. B. KOHLER-KOCH (1997), *The European Union facing enlargement: still a system sui generis?*, MZES Working Papers, No. 50.

131. P. R. KRUGMAN (1979), *A model of balance-of-payments crises*, Journal of Money, Credit, and Banking, 11, pp. 311–325.

132. L. LIPSCHITZ, T. LANE, AND A. MOURMOURAS (2001), *Capital flows to transition economies: master or servant*, IMF Working Paper, No. 11.

133. A. LOWE (1965), *Politische Ökonomie: Geschichte und Kritik*, Europa, Vienna.

134. ——(1987), *Essays in political economics. Public control in a democratic society*, Harvester Press, Brighton, Sussex.

135. J. G. MARCH AND J. P. OLSON (1984), *The new institutionalism: organizational factors in political life*, American Political Science Review, 78, pp. 734–749.

136. G. MARINI AND G. PIERSANTI (2001), *Fiscal deficits and currency crises*, Departmental Working Papers from Tor Vergata University, No. 140.

137. R. I. MCKINNON (1991), *Liberalizing foreign trade in a socialist economy: the problem of negative value added*, in: Currency Convertibility in Eastern Europe, J. Williamson, ed., Institute for International Economics, Washington, DC, pp. 96–115.

138. E. G. MENDOZA AND M. URIBE (1999), *Devaluation risk and the syndrome of exchange-rate-based stabilizations*, NBER Working Paper, No. 7014.

139. A. MERLO AND C. WILSON (1995), *A stochastic model of sequential bargaining with complete information*, Econometrica, 63, pp. 371–399.

140. H. V. MILNER (1997), *Interests, institutions and information: domestic politics and international relations*, Princeton University Press, Princeton, NJ.

141. J. MILYO (2000), *Logical deficiencies in spatial models: a constructive critique*, Public Choice, 105, pp. 273–289.

142. ——(2000), *A problem with Euclidean preferences in spatial models of politics*, Economic Letters, 66, pp. 179–182.

143. F. S. MISHKIN (1999), *Lessons from the Asian crises*, NBER Working Paper, No. 7102.

144. ——(2000), *Inflation targeting in emerging-market countries*, American Economic Review, 90, pp. 105–109.

145. A. MORAVCSIK (1993), *Preferences and power in the European community: a liberal intergovernmentalist approach*, Journal of Common Market Studies, 31, pp. 473–524.

146. ——(1997), *Taking preferences seriously: a liberal theory of internations politics*, International Organization, 51, pp. 513–553.

147. ——(1998), *The choice of Europe. Social purpose and state power from Messina to Maastricht*, Cornell University Press, Ithaca, New York.

148. H. MOULIN (1982), *Game theory for the social sciences*, New York University Press, New York, NY.

149. A. MUTHOO (1999), *Bargaining theory with applications*, Cambridge University Press, Cambridge, MA.

150. J. F. NASH (1950), *The bargaining problem*, Econometrica, 18, pp. 155–162.

151. ——(1953), *Two-person cooperative games*, Econometrica, 21, pp. 128–140.

152. F. M. NATALUCCI AND F. RAVENNA (2002), *The road to adopting the Euro: monetary policy and exchange rate regimes in EU candidate countries*, Board of Governors of the Federal Reserve System - International Finance Discussion Papers, No. 741.

153. C. J. NEELY AND C. J. WALLER (1997), *A benefit cost analysis of disinflation*, Contemporary Economic Policy, 5, pp. 50–64.

154. D. C. NORTH (1990), *Institutions, institutional change and economic performance*, Cambridge University Press, Cambridge, MA.

155. D. M. NUTI (2002), *Costs and benefits of unilateral euroisation in Central Eastern Europe*, Russian-European Centre for Economic Policy Working Paper Series.

156. M. OBSTFELD (1995), *Models of currency crises with self-fulfilling features*, NBER Working Paper, No. 5285.

157. OECD (2000), *Economic outlook*, OECD Economic Outlook (December).

158. M. OLSON (1965), *The logic of collective action*, Harvard University Press, Cambridge, MA.

159. R. PAHRE (1997), *Endogenous domestic institutions in two-level games and parliamentary oversight of the European Union*, Journal of Conflict Resolution, 41, pp. 147–174.

160. F. U. PAPPI (1996), *Political behavior: reasoning voters and multi-party systems*, in: A New Handbook of Political Science, R. E. Goodin and H.-D. Klingemann, eds., Oxford University Press, Oxford, pp. 255–275.

161. T. PERSSON (2001), *Do political institutions shape economic policy?*, NBER Working Paper, No. 8214.

162. T. PERSSON AND G. TABELLINI (2000), *Political economics: explaining economic policy*, MIT Press, Cambridge, MA.

163. T. PLÜMPER (1995), *Quasi-rationale Akteure und die Funktion internationaler Institutionen*, Zeitschrift für Internationale Beziehungen, 2, pp. 49–77.

164. M. A. POLLACK (2001), *International relations theory and European integration*, Journal of Common Market Studies, 39, pp. 221–244.

165. K. R. POPPER (1994), *The myth of the framework: in defence of science and rationality*, Routledge, New York, NY.

166. R. POWELL (1989), *The dynamics of longer brinkmanship crises*, in: Models of Strategic Choice in Politics, P. C. Ordeshook, ed., University of Michigan Press, Ann Arbor.

167. R. D. PUTNAM (1988), *Diplomacy and domestic politics: the logic of two-level games*, International Organization, 42, pp. 427–460.

168. J. RAHN (2003), *Bilateral equilibrium exchange rates of EU accession countries against the Euro*, BOFIT Discussion Papers, No. 11.

169. P. ROBSON (1998), *The economics of international integration*, Routledge, London and New York, 4 ed.

170. P. M. ROMER (1994), *The origins of endogenous growth theory*, Journal of Economic Perspectives, 8, pp. 3–22.

171. K. ROSS AND A. UBIDE (2001), *Mind the gap: what is the best measure of slack in the Euro area*, IMF Working Paper, No. 203.

172. J. ROSTOWSKI (2002), *The Eastern enlargement of the EU and the case for unilateral euroization*, mimeo.

173. A. E. ROTH (1979), *Axiomatic models of bargaining*, Springer, Berlin, Heidelberg, New York.

174. A. RUBINSTEIN (1982), *Perfect equilibrium in a bargaining model*, Econometrica, 50, pp. 97–110.

175. G. SAINT-PAUL (2000), *The "new political economy": recent books by Allen Drazen and by Torsten Persson and Guido Tabellini*, Journal of Economic Literature, 38, pp. 915–925.

176. P. A. SAMUELSON (1964), *Theoretical notes on trade problems*, Review of Economics and Statistics, 23, pp. 1–60.

177. W. SANDHOLTZ (1996), *Membership matters: limits of the functional approach to European institutions*, Journal of Common Market Studies, 34, pp. 403–429.

178. W. SANDHOLTZ AND J. ZYSMAN (1989), *1992: Recasting the European bargain*, World Politics, 47, pp. 95–128.

179. T. C. SCHELLING (1960), *Strategy of conflict*, Harvard University Press, Cambridge, MA.

180. F. SCHIMMELFENNIG (2001), *The community trap: liberal norms, rhetorical action, and the Eastern enlargement of the European Union*, International Organization, 55, pp. 47–80.

181. C. SCHMIDT (1994), *Preferences, beliefs, knowledge and crisis in the international decision-making process: a theoretical approach through qualitative games*, in: Game Theory and International Relations, P. Allan and C. Schmidt, eds., Edward Elgar, Adlershot, pp. 97–122.

182. G. SCHNEIDER (2002), *A never-ending success story? The dynamics of widening and deepening European integration*, in: Widening the European Union: the politics of institutional change and reform, B. Steunenberg, ed., Routledge, London, pp. 183–201.

183. G. SCHNEIDER AND L.-E. CEDERMAN (1994), *The change of tide in political cooperation: a limeted information model of European integration*, International Organization, 48, pp. 633–662.

184. J. A. SCHUMPETER (1944), *Capitalism, socialism, and democracy*, George Allan and Unwin, London.

185. R. SCHWEICKERT (2001), *Assessing the advantages of EMU-enlargement for the EU and the accession countries: a comparative indicator approach*, Kiel Working Paper, No. 1080.

186. K. A. SHEPSLE AND B. R. WEINGAST (1984), *Political solutions to market problems*, American Political Science Review, 78, pp. 417–434.

187. H. SIEBERT (2002), *An iron law of currency crises: the divergence of the nominal and the real exchange rate and increasing current account deficits*, Kiel Working Paper, No. 1106.

188. H. A. SIMON (1982), *Models of bounded rationality*, MIT Press, Cambridge, MA.

189. K.-H. SIMON (2000), *Criteria of systems performance from a macrosociological viewpoint*, in: The Performance of Social Systems, F. Parra-Luna, ed., Kluwer Academic/Plenum Publishers, The Hague, Boston, London, pp. 131–146.

190. H.-W. SINN AND M. REUTTER (2001), *The minimum inflation rate for euroland*, NBER Working Paper, No. 8085.

191. H. SJURSEN (2002), *Why expand? the question of legitimacy and justification in the EU's enlargement policy*, Journal of Common Market Studies, 40, pp. 491–513.

192. I. STÅHL (1972), *Bargaining theory*, EFI, Economic Research Institute, Stockholm.

193. A. A. STEIN (1982), *Coordination and collaboration: regimes in an anarchic world*, International Organization, 36, pp. 299–324.

194. B. STEUNENBERG (2002), *An ever wider union: the effects of enlargement on EU decision-making*, in: Widening the European Union: the politics of institutional change and reform, B. Steunenberg, ed., Routledge, London, pp. 97–118.

195. B. STEUNENBERG, D. SCHMIDTCHEN, AND C. KOBOLDT (1999), *Strategic power in the European Union: evaluating the distribution of power in policy games*, Journal of Theoretical Politics, 11, pp. 339–366.

196. M. SUTTER (2000), *Flexible integration, EMU and relative voting power in the EU*, Public Choice, 104, pp. 41–62.

197. G. SZAPÁRY (2001), *Maastricht and the choice of exchange rate regime in transition countries during the run-up to EMU*, ENEPRI Working Paper, No. 6.

198. R. D. TOLLISON AND T. D. WILLETT (1979), *An economic theory of mutually advantageous issue linkages in international negotiations*, International Organization, 33, pp. 425–449.

199. A. TORNELL AND A. VELASCO (1995), *Money-based versus exchange rate-based stabilization with endogenous fiscal policy*, NBER Working Paper, No. 5300.

200. G. TSEBELIS (1990), *Nested games: rational choice in comparative politics*, University of California Press, Berkely, CA.

201. ——(1995), *Decision making in political systems: veto players in presidentialism, parliamentarism, multicameralism und multipartyism*, British Journal of Political Science, 25, pp. 289–325.

202. L. TSOUKALIS (1997), *The new European economy revisited*, Oxford University Press, Oxford, 3 ed.

203. J. A. TUCKER, A. C. PACEK, AND A. J. BERINSKY (2002), *Transitional winners and losers: attitudes toward EU membership in post-communist countries*, American Journal of Political Science, 46, pp. 557–571.

204. R. H. WAGNER (1989), *Uncerainty, rational learning, and bargaining in the Cuban missile crisis*, in: Models of Strategic Choice in Politics, P. C. Ordeshook, ed., University of Michigan Press, Ann Arbor, pp. 177–205.

205. K. WALLNER (2003), *Specific investments and the EU enlargement*, Journal of Public Economics, 87, pp. 867–882.

206. W. WEIDLICH (1989), *Stability and cyclicity in social systems*, in: Dissipative Strukturen in Integrierten Systemen, A. B. Çambel, B. Fritsch, and J. U. Keller, eds., Nomos, Baden-Baden, pp. 193–222.

207. B. R. WEINGAST (1996), *Political institutions: rational choice perspectives*, in: A New Handbook of Political Science, R. E. Goodin and H.-D. Klingemann, eds., Oxford University Press, Oxford, pp. 167–189.

208. J. R. WESTBROOK AND T. D. WILLETT (1999), *Exchange rates as nominal anchors: an overview of the issues*, in: Exchange-Rate Policies for Emerging Market Economies, R. J. Sweeny, C. G. Wihlborg, and T. D. Willett, eds., Westview Press, Boulder, CL, pp. 83–112.

209. T. D. WILLETT (2000), *Some political economy aspects of EMU*, Journal of Policy Modelling, 22, pp. 379–389.

210. ———(2001), *The political economy of external discipline: constraint versus incentive effects of capital mobility and exchange rate pegs*, mimeo.

211. M. B. WILLIAMS (2003), *From Copenhagen (1993) to Copenhagen (2002): the Eastern enlargement in comparative perspective*, mimeo.

212. O. E. WILLIAMSON (2000), *The new institutional economics: taking stock, looking ahead*, Journal of Economic Literature, 38, pp. 595–613.

213. C. WÓJCIK (2000), *A critical review of unilateral euroization proposals: the case of Poland*, Focus on Transition, 2, pp. 48–76.

214. D. WOLF AND B. ZANGL (1996), *The European Economic and Monetary Union: 'two-level games' and the formation of international relations*, European Journal of International Relations, 2, pp. 355–393.

Printing: Krips bv, Meppel
Binding: Stürtz, Würzburg